SIMPLY FLOWERS

à Amsterdam
chez S.J. BAALDE,
à Utrecht
chez B. WILD

Also by Barbara Milo Ohrbach

The Scented Room

The Scented Room Gardening Notebook

Antiques at Home

A Token of Friendship

Memories of Childhood

A Bouquet of Flowers

A Cheerful Heart

The Spirit of America

Merry Christmas

3

Mart. Engelbrecht excud. A.V.

1371

BARBARA MILO OHRBACH

SIMPLY FLOWERS

PRACTICAL ADVICE
AND BEAUTIFUL IDEAS
FOR CREATING
FLOWER-FILLED ROOMS

PHOTOGRAPHS BY JOHN HALL

Clarkson Potter/Publishers
NEW YORK

Publisher's Note: This book contains several recipes using botanicals.
Some of these may cause allergic reactions in some individuals,
so reasonable care in preparation is advised.

Published by Clarkson N. Potter, Inc., 201 East 50th Street, New York,
New York, 10022. Member of the Crown Publishing Group.
Random House, Inc. New York, Toronto, London, Sydney, Auckland

CLARKSON N. POTTER, POTTER and colophon are trademarks of
Clarkson N. Potter, Inc.

Manufactured in Japan

Design by Rochelle Udell and Robert Valentine

Library of Congress Cataloging-in-Publication Data
Ohrbach, Barbara Milo.
Simply flowers: practical advice and beautiful ideas for creating
flower-filled rooms / Barbara Milo Ohrbach : photographs by John Hall.
p. cm.
Includes index.
1. Flower arrangement.   2. Flowers.   3. Flower arrangement—Pictorial works.
4. Flowers—Pictorial works.   I. Title.
SB449.045   1993
745.92—dc20   92-29768
CIP
ISBN 0-517-58183-3

10 9 8 7 6 5 4 3 2 1
First Edition

*"The simple flowers
of our spring are what I
want to see again."*
JOHN KEATS

This book is dedicated to anyone
with a passion for flowers,
and to the idea that now,
more than ever, we must try
to sustain the fragile presence of flowers
and
all growing things in our world.

ACKNOWLEDGMENTS

It is with much affection and gratitude that I acknowledge the cooperation of everyone listed on these pages. They have all made my working on *Simply Flowers* a joyful experience!

Fond thank-you's to a wonderful group—my exceptional editor, Shirley Wohl, for her caring and competent attention at all times; my photographer, John Hall for his dedication, and gentlemanly ways; Rochelle Udell, my designer, for her remarkable talent and willingness to change "a little something" with a smile; my agent, Deborah Geltman, who is always ready, willing and able to do whatever needs to be done, especially during the three years I worked on this book; and Charles Acree, Beth Allen, Gayle Benderoff, Anne Marie Cloutier, Lisa Fresne, Patricia O'Leary, Jane Rappeport, Sarah Williams Thomas, Jane Treuhaft, and Robert Valentine—much appreciation for their hard work and enthusiasm.

I would especially like to acknowledge these people at Clarkson Potter/Crown, my publisher. Through their teamwork and problem solving, they have made all my books, including this one, a beautiful reality—María Bottino,

Cathy Collins, Joan Denman, Jo Fagen, Phyllis Fleiss, Lisa Keim, Howard Klein, Barbara Marks, Matthew Mayer, Bill Nave, Teresa Nicholas, Ed Otto, Pam Romano, Lauren Shakely, Michelle Sidrane, Carol Southern, Laurie Stark, Robin Strashun, and Helen Zimmermann.

Particular thanks to all the notable floral designers listed here. Their precious talents and outstanding ways with flowers are woven throughout—Rita Bobry, Spring St. Garden; Pat Braun and Stephen Lilie, Salou; Zezé Calvo and Peggy O'Dea, Zezé; Robert Day, Robert Day Flowers, Ltd.; Caroline Dickenson, Caroline Dickenson Flowers; J. Barry Ferguson, J. Barry Ferguson, Ltd.; Angela Flanders, The Flower Room; Lisa Krieger, Lisa Krieger Gardens and Interiors; Mary Mahaffey, The Millbrook Village Flower Shoppe; Jane Packer, Jane Packer Floral Design; Tom Prichard and Billy Jarecki, Pure Mädderlake; K. W. C. Pymer, T. and E. Page, Covent Garden; Renny Reynolds, Renny; Sarah Reynolds, Sarah Reynolds Flowers; Jill Warren and Sheila Taylor-Jones, Edward Goodyear, Ltd.; Sonja Waites, Pulbrook & Gould, Ltd.; and Jayne Yianni, Jane Packer Flower School.

I am also indebted to all the gracious people who shared their love of flowers and hospitality with me—Richard Clegg; Joanna Cooper and Susan Moody of the Cloisters; Val Cridland and Jubilee House; Maxime Hoff, Silk Flower Arrangements; Harold Koda and The Edward C. Blum Laboratory at F.I.T.; Charles Masson and Gisele Masson of La Grenouille; Rosemary Nicholson and The Museum of Garden History; Clare Potter; Mr. & Ms. Jack Quartararo; Vivienne Scott and The Royal Horticultural Society; Mr. and Mrs. Dave Neilson and the Salisbury Garden Center; and Maison Trousselier. Thank you, also, to Clare Ascavi, Ms. Arthur De Garis, Devereus Ltd. Antiques, Kari and Liz Haavisto, Kevin Di Martine, Vie and Al Koerner, Mary Maguire, Christine Mulholland, Samuel Mintz Straus, Helen Panos, Margery and Charles Sadowsky, Pat Sadowsky, Tonny Salvato, Sheila Sanders, Dennis Stone, Michael Sureda, Treasure Chest, Peter Watkins, and Toni Wing.

And, just to belie poet Ogden Nash's humorous remark that flower arrangements can sometimes lead to marital discord, I'd like to thank my dear husband, Mel, who has been replenishing the water in the vases in our house for twenty-three years.

TABLE OF

CONTENTS

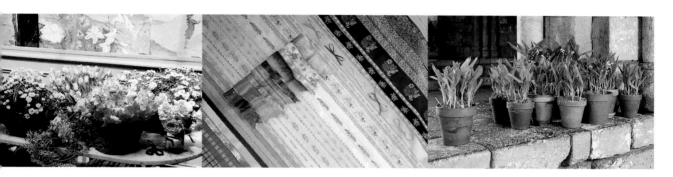

INTRO

DUCTION

I recently visited Appledore Island in New Hampshire, something I have always wanted to do. This is where the nineteenth-century writer and poet Celia Thaxter planted her famous cutting garden, which has now been restored. As we approached the island, we could see a patchwork quilt of flowers springing from the jagged rocks. That the garden has survived is a reassuring reminder of the significance of flowers.

In Celia Thaxter's book *An Island Garden* (reissued in 1978), there is a short passage that reflects what flowers mean to me: "Ever since I could remember anything, flowers have been like dear friends to me, comforters, inspirers, powers to uplift and cheer."

For many of us, flowers seem to call up our fondest memories. I'll never forget the bouquet of flowers (almost bigger than I was) given to me at age six after a ballet recital. Or the wrist corsage that was sent on the afternoon of my Junior Prom—a real, live orchid! Even now, I can remember what those flowers looked like and the wonderful feeling I had when I received them.

Flowers celebrate joyful occasions

such as birthdays, weddings, and graduations, and console us in less happy times. They're also presented as tributes to accomplishment and as expressions of welcome and hospitality.

But more than anything else, I think that flowers symbolize hope. No matter how uncertain our world sometimes seems, we can count on flowers to appear each spring, an unfailing reminder of the cycle of nature and its precious bounty. We must continually remind ourselves not to take them for granted. I'm not alone in this idea. Although I read *The Naval Treaty* by Arthur Conan Doyle as a child, I recently came across this very interesting (and uncharacteristic) passage from it in which Sherlock Holmes says:

Our highest assurance of the goodness of Providence seems to me to rest in the flowers. All other things, our powers, our desires, our food, are really necessary for our existence in the first instance. But this rose is an extra. Its smell and its color are an embellishment of life, not a condition of it. It is only goodness which gives extras, and so I say again that we have much to hope from the flowers.

Beautiful things are enduring and should matter to all of us. We should stop and smell the flowers more often. There is something very worthwhile in trying to recapture the sense of wonder that we had in childhood and in striving for simple contentment. One way I do this is by working with flowers and filling my home with them.

ᐤ OVERLEAF: Family snapshots on my bulletin board show the work put into the garden over the years—and all the joys and gifts it has given back to us.

ᐤ OPPOSITE: This clear pink beauty is a Prairie Princess rose that is growing on the trellis in our cutting garden.

Since the publication of *The Scented Room,* my book on dried flowers and potpourris, so many of you have written to say how it has inspired and enabled you to accomplish something you never thought you could do. Some of you even suggested that I write a book on arranging fresh flowers, with an easy-to-follow unpretentious approach to the subject. I became enthusiastic about this idea, and I hope you like the result.

My philosophy is this: stop worrying about what you don't know, and just start working with the flowers. Because we all lead such busy lives, we want to use our free time in pursuits that are gratifying, not drudgery. I always want to feel good about whatever I'm doing and to be able to deal with it in a straightforward way. This is also my approach to arranging flowers.

It seems to me that there are too many rules, which could intimidate people who have limited experience. After all, at times, we just want to make simple bouquets with a minimum of fuss. True, there are certain basics to every art, and flower arranging is no exception. But for this book I have tried to streamline them, making them comfortable to read and absorb. There are recommendations to those of you just starting out, as well as reminders for those who are more experienced. And I've included some new ideas and creative approaches for everyone to try. My objective has been to make flower arranging easy and enjoyable.

Some people have a knack for doing things. Everything they touch has style and looks as if it were professionally done. Although one is born with a knack, most of us can still have fun and get good results arranging flowers. Just developing self-confidence can help you to create something beautiful. When working with flowers, there are untold ways in which to express yourself, and you'll find that the possibilities are limitless.

🌿 The picture above was taken while we were photographing abroad for part of this book. Many of the street corners, like this one in London, are filled with flower stalls continually offering brilliant displays of color and enormous variety.

❧ I celebrated my birthday while working in London, so my thoughtful husband called florist Pulbrook & Gould from New York, and had these glorious flowers sent to me. They filled my hotel room with sweet beauty and fragrance for days.

Simply Flowers covers many aspects of working with and arranging fresh flowers. The book includes a short history of flowers and their influence on the decorative and fine arts; suggestions for placing flowers in your home and for decorating your tables for dining and entertaining; new ideas for containers and vases; instructions on preparing and arranging your botanicals in a sensible and efficient way; and how to make gifts of flowers even more beautiful. In addition, there are special lists of the best flowers, herbs, branches, and grasses, and colorful fruits and vegetables to use in your arrangements, as well as fragrant-flower ideas and clever recipes. Since so many people like potted plants as well as cut flowers in their homes, I've included a section on this subject that also covers forcing bulbs and branches. And for those times when cut flowers aren't available, some possible alternatives such as silk and porcelain flowers are discussed.

Because the quality of the flowers you choose for arrangements is so important, the last chapter of the book is my guide to where you can find the best botanicals—from greengrocers and outdoor markets to the finest florists. I interviewed some of the top floral designers here and abroad and have included tips from them as well as photographs of their creations. Flower gardens and other flower essentials are also discussed. And finally, there is a Source Directory in which I share the names, addresses, and phone numbers of all my favorite places to obtain cut flowers, seeds, bulbs, plants, tools, and supplies; my personal list of garden and flower book authors (both past and contemporary); and the names of societies you can join to enhance your knowledge and enjoyment of flowers.

I envisioned *Simply Flowers* as an intimate conversation, and so I decided to use the common or familiar names of flowers. As you work with the flowers, chances are you'll want to know more about them and start to master the Latin names on your own. Vita Sackville-West wryly addresses this subject in her book *Passenger to Teheran:*

...for I am not sure that pure enjoyment does not wane as technical knowledge waxes; I am tempted to put it to the test, by studying botany till I can distinguish Scrophulariaceae from Caryophyllaceae, but that I am too much afraid of finding, when I have digested all this knowledge, that I have lost the delights of ignorance.

And although she knew more about flowers than any of us probably ever will, I find the sense of her remarks appealing. It's the old-fashioned and charming names of flowers—like buttercup, forget-me-not, johnny-jump-up, and morning glory—that have a special power to con-

My niece and nephew harvesting Silver King artemesia, lavender, pot marjoram, and thyme in our verdant herb garden on a hot summer day. Their love of gardening is a family trait that we hope will be passed on to their own children. (Isn't that a sweet thought?)

nect us to the past and to the simple people who originated these names for the flowers they first grew so long ago.

It can be very gratifying to handle and tend to flowers. And if you are fortunate enough to have your own garden, flowers become a part of your life. Years ago, when my husband and I first bought our country house, my mother laughed and asked me what we were going to do with all the land. I wish she could see it now, almost two decades later.

It has become a gathering place for our extended family. The trees and shrubs that my mother and father helped us put in are now almost fully grown, as are the nieces and nephews who, as children often do, took naturally to gardening, helping us plant seeds, label herbs, and harvest lavender (at 10¢ a bunch, now a family joke). They have become a part of everything that grows in this enchanted garden of their childhood. In fact, my niece D. J., who as a teenager always had to be roped into helping, recently wrote to us from Bolivia, where she is with the Peace Corps, that she is teaching the villagers how to garden! The love of plants that my parents and grandparents instilled in us is now touching yet another generation in our family.

As I write this, I can smell the lilacs in bloom outside my window. They are old-fashioned white ones, fragrant and voluptuous, planted long before we moved here. Looking out, I see the wisteria draped around trees in the woods, where pink and white dogwoods flower against the deep green.

The herb garden is now surrounded with graceful bridal wreath and a hedge of yews. Sweet thyme winds its way between the stones on the terrace, which is bordered by fragrant and edible herbs. And growing everywhere are old-fashioned roses, the thickest clusters climbing the stone walls and spilling down the steps leading to the vegetable garden and our new flower garden.

The vegetable garden was planted

❧ Some views of our cutting/flower garden at various stages of growth. Here's how it looks in early spring when the perennials have just started to peek through the soil. (The fence wasn't just a pretty addition, but a necessity for keeping the rabbits from nibbling the flowers!)

❧ That's me in the garden as it looks in midsummer. Everything is finally planted, but by this stage the weeding is continuous. A garden is hard work, but like almost anything worthwhile, ultimately rewarding. Our lush, old-fashioned roses, just starting to bloom, are proof.

❧ By the time August arrives, everyone in the family pitches in because there is so much to do. Besides weeding and watering and cutting blossoms for arranging in vases around the house, we must stake the stems of some of them because they've grown so big and tall.

🐚 I love flowers in every room of the house, especially in summer. Below left is a country basket filled with flowers just picked from the garden. The arrangement, below right, includes peonies, delphinium, roses, allium, lupine, bellflowers, and wild roses—also picked from our garden, to create a welcoming note in the hall.

🐚 ABOVE LEFT: I even wear flowers around my neck in this bud-vase pendant! ABOVE RIGHT: Here I am relaxing, next to our rose-laced trellis. OPPOSITE: A favorite picture of my grandparents. My grandmother is holding a large bouquet of the same type of sweetheart roses that fill the little silver vase on this unique old frame.

the year after we bought the house, and its produce is something we look forward to each summer. We've just added some new plants—flowering kale, colorful peppers, and tiny tomatoes—to use in our flower arrangements. There's a prolific raspberry patch on one side and strawberries grow on the other.

The flower garden shown on these pages and in Chapter 5 has proved to be a wonderful addition. I can really indulge myself now, and for the first time, cut *all* the flowers I want. The back gate of the flower garden opens into the orchard, where the fruit and nut trees—apple, peach, plum, pear, and pecan—sometimes flower all at once. When I'm working in the garden, I watch the bees busily going about their work, a glorious sight, and I am reminded of the important role flowers play in nature.

The garden has evolved over the years. It also changes daily—mornings, evenings, after a cooling rain, and of course, during the various seasons. But for me, it always remains a sanctuary, a happy place where I can go, as Celia Thaxter says here, for continual renewal.

When in these fresh mornings I go into my garden before anyone is awake, I go for the time being into perfect happiness . . . the fair face of every flower salutes me with a silent joy that fills me with infinite content.

It is this contentment that is with us when we are working with flowers and brightening our lives with them. Their very colors and fragrances give us a lift. And we should not overlook their value in the workplace or the sickroom.

Appreciation of the gifts of nature goes a lot deeper than we may think. I've come to believe more strongly than ever that it's the little things that make life more meaningful, and that give us the strength to deal with the complicated problems that come along.

While individually we may not be able to resolve the world's problems, perhaps the world would be a nicer place in which to live if we all valued flowers more, and remembered that they are part of a much larger picture. As John Gerard said in the seventeenth century, "who would look up dangerously at planets that might look safely down at plants?" When you bring flowers into your home and your life, you surround your family and friends with natural beauty that creates a climate of well-being and continuity. Flowers are essential. In many ways, we cannot survive without them.

Barbara Milo Ohrbach

THE WORLD

# of Flowers

CHAPTER

Flowers surround us, even in rooms where there are no fresh flowers. Just take a few moments now to look around you. If your home is anything like mine, flowers are strewn on the fabrics that cover the beds, windows, and pillows. Printed on engravings or carved into the wood that frames them. And adorn the furniture and the many small objects that make a house so warm and comfortable. Once we become aware of them, we suddenly realize that flowers are everywhere, peeking at us from teacups and silver spoons, giving pleasure from day to day, all year round.

Why are we drawn to flowers? Why do most of us love all things green and growing, sometimes with a passion that defies logic? Why do flowers make us feel so happy? One explanation is that their natural beauty touches a number of senses at once—delighting the eye with endless varieties of form and color; tantalizing the

nose and awakening memory with their evocative scents; inviting the tentative touch of a fingertip on a velvety petal.

Artist Georgia O'Keeffe once said this about the flowers she so sensuously painted: "Everyone has many associations with a flower—the idea of flowers. You put out your hand to touch the flower—lean forward to smell it—maybe touch it with your lips almost without thinking—or give it to someone to please them." The appeal of both living flowers and the flower motif in decorative and all other forms of art is universal and timeless.

Flowers celebrate, console, cheer. From ancient Chinese scroll paintings and Egyptian bas-relief, the earliest civilizations enjoyed flowers, using them to show esteem, and to mark celebrations and rites of passage. The early Persians and Romans were serious gardeners who cultivated many flowers, especially roses, for their homes and special festivities.

And later, in Europe during the Middle Ages, the Church actively supported horticulture. Most monasteries had large orchards and kitchen gardens. The beauty of the herbs and flowers, grown for their medicinal properties, would inevitably inspire designs and borders for the illumination of manuscripts that were so painstakingly painted by the monks. (A fine collection of these is in the Pierpont Morgan Library in New York City.)

Cut flowers in vases were first depicted in the paintings of the Renaissance. By the sixteenth century, new plants were being introduced into Europe. The great

❧ OVERLEAF: A charming nineteenth-century oil painting that I found many years ago. I still love looking at it.
❧ ABOVE: Garden flowers in an old urn painted in miniature, an embroidered ribbon, and a delphinium-filled cobalt blue vase on a background of richly woven gold Italian silk damask cloth.
❧ BELOW: A beadwork sewing kit in the shape of a book depicts cottage garden flowers. It sits on a wool shawl, circa 1850, strewn with big cabbage roses.

13

❦ ABOVE LEFT: A brass statue from the nineteenth century shows a goddess perched on a lion's back holding a cornucopia overflowing with bounty from the garden.

❦ ABOVE RIGHT: Flowers everywhere—a Victorian day book with *petit point* roses; a Bilston enamel bodkin case painted with tiny pink buds; a round snuff box with a floral brass inset; a delicate ivory miniature; a brass plaque embossed with a perfect rose; under it all, a flower-filled urn on an old needlepoint seat cover.

❦ BELOW LEFT: Old-fashioned pitchers are just right when you have a few fresh flowers. Here, an English Coalport jug holds a Gloriosa lily and a pale pink rose.

❦ BELOW RIGHT: The rose, tulip, and anemone at their best on an Italian shell cameo.

⥻ ABOVE LEFT: Garland-bearing cherubs dancing on an old marble fountain—one of the many wonderful things to be seen at the Museum of Gardening in London.

⥻ ABOVE RIGHT: A jeweled flower pin fashioned from a gold Victorian thimble and gemstones. In the seventeenth and eighteenth centuries, the "Language of Flowers," used in jewelry, became an everlasting way of expressing love and affection.

⥻ BELOW LEFT: I love collecting antique handkerchiefs lavishly embellished with embroidery and lace—especially when the motif includes flowers like these.

⥻ BELOW RIGHT: A cornucopia bedpost with fruits and flowers in the Empress Josephine's bedroom—one of the restored imperial rooms at the Château de Compiègne.

maritime powers, England, Holland, and Italy, vied for the treasures found in far-off lands. And part of the booty they brought back were botanical specimens. Before long, botanists, scientists, and horticulturists began cultivating these new finds for study in their own gardens, and people began making permanent records of their transient beauty on paper.

Many of these were produced in the seventeenth and eighteenth centuries as books containing engravings and illustrations of rare detail and elegance—like those by John Parkinson, Basil Besler, G. D. Ehret, Elizabeth Blackwell, William Curtis, and Dr. Robert Thornton. Carl Linnaeus, the eighteenth-century Swedish botanist who established the system for classifying plants, seems to sum up the primary motivation of these botanical artists: "All for the love of flowers." (If you have botanical engravings hanging on the walls of your home and they are nineteenth-century or earlier, they are probably from old books.)

The awakening interest in botany also sparked the fashion for interior flower decoration—but not always in the form of real flowers. In fact, in seventeenth-century Holland, at the same time that tulipomania saw some people mortgaging their homes in order to purchase rare tulip bulbs, others were substituting fresh flower arrangements with elaborate paintings of them to brighten their gloomy Dutch interiors. And what paintings they were! Lush still lifes brimming with such naturalistic details, masterfully painted to the last dew drop on a petal. The style, beginning with such Dutch and Flemish artists as Jan Brueghel, Rachel

Ruysch, and Jan van Huysum, spread, especially to France with Jean-Baptiste Monnoyer, Jean-Baptiste-Siméon Chardin, and François Boucher painting flowers and arrangements that we still look to today for inspiration and ideas.

On both sides of the Channel, flowers were bursting forth in other forms as well. A 1688 inventory of Burghley, one of my favorite English country houses, lists thirty-seven bunches of solid silver flowers for table decoration (used, perhaps, in autumn and winter). Books on how to use flowers indoors began to appear. Floral motifs were sprouting up on wood carvings by Grinling Gibbons. On

tapestries from Gobelin and Beauvais. On porcelain from Sèvres and Meissen. And on everything else from hand-painted fans to furniture, much of it inspired by such great rococo artists as Jean Honoré Fragonard and Jean Antoine Watteau, whose flower-drenched paintings presaged the dawn of romanticism.

This infatuation with naturalism was destined to cool somewhat with the arrival of nineteenth-century neoclassicism. But from 1802 to 1824, Pierre Joseph Redouté produced his two now-famous series of prints, Les Liliacées, 500 hand-colored engravings of lilies and related flowers, and Les Roses, in which the roses that grew in Empress Josephine's garden at Malmaison are forever preserved. By 1837, when Queen Victoria ascended the British throne and made respectability and family life fashionable, domestic and decorative arts flourished with the flower motif as a favorite subject. An English city merchant could satisfy his longing for rural life with porcelain figurines depicting country pursuits. And when tea was served, he was likely to sip it from flower-painted cups provided by Wedgwood.

Shopkeepers did a brisk business in flower-bedecked ribbons, lace, textiles,

and embroidery, while artisans worked an endless variety of blooms into all manner of materials, like ceramics, wood, metal, marble, and ivory. And at a time when every imaginable flower was endowed with its own sentimental symbolism (pansies for thought, roses for love, and so on), it seemed only natural to transfer the popular "Language of Flowers" into enduring tokens of jewelry.

It was in the Victorian era that horticulture and flower arranging reached their peak. *Godey's Lady's Book* and Mrs. Beeton's *Book of Household Management* considered the act of arranging flowers itself a morally uplifting pastime.

The late nineteenth and early twentieth centuries saw the beginning of a trend in publishing on gardening and flowers in the United States and England that continues unabated today. Books by Alice Morse Earle, Gertrude Jekyll, Jane Webb Loudon, William Robinson, Celia Thaxter, Edith Wharton, and others are still a source of inspiration. (At the end of this book, I have included a list of garden and flower writers, past and present, whom I particularly admire.)

Claude Monet once said: "I perhaps owe having become a painter to flowers." The accumulated legacy that flowers have left to the arts can still be seen and enjoyed by us today in art galleries and museums. Who can pick a batch of sunflowers without thinking of Vincent van Gogh? Or arrange a vase of roses without picturing how they were painted by Henri Fantin-Latour or photographed by Edward Steichen? Paul Cezanne, Odilon Redon, Pierre Auguste Renoir, Childe Hassam—we can learn so much from their creative genius.

Whenever I'm in such exceptional flower gardens as those of the Bagatelle or Giverny in France, or the restored gardens at Thomas Jefferson's Monticello, or Betrix Farrand's sunken garden at Hill-Stead in Connecticut, I am always amazed at how differently people are inspired by flowers. And, of course, I can't wait to return home and try a few new ideas myself! Because it always comes back to this —the precious beauty of living flowers, and the certainty that we can count on them, spring after spring, to renew our spirits and brighten our homes.

🐚 **THIS PAGE: This extraordinary imperial enamel egg, entwined with gold and pearl lilies-of-the-valley, was made by Fabergé for the Russian royal family. It is now in the Forbes Museum.**
🐚 **OPPOSITE: A miniature garden of real lilies-of-the-valley growing in a lovely eighteenth-century French jardinière.**

FLOWER-FIL

LED ROOMS

CHAPTER 2

China tea, the scent of hyacinths, wood fires, and bowls of violets—that is my mental picture of an agreeable February afternoon.

These wonderful words from Constance Spry, the English doyenne of modern flower arrangers, echo my own feeling about flower-filled rooms. Nothing so instantly lifts the spirit as the presence of live, growing things. For me, they're practically a necessity. That's why our house is always filled with vases of flowers and baskets of fruits and vegetables. There's always a jelly glass on my kitchen counter where I can plunk the latest offerings from the garden.

A room is transformed when you introduce something green and growing from the outdoors. Suddenly, it becomes warmer, friendlier, more comfortable—a room where people love to be. And this is true whether you live in a country house or a city apartment.

Get in the habit of bringing the outdoors in. Flowers in the living and dining rooms, of course. But how about a small vase on your desk, on a bathroom vanity, or in a guest room—even if you're not expecting any! One of the things I love about Europe is the sight of people rushing home for lunch with a loaf of bread under one arm and a fresh bouquet in the other. For them, flowers are a part of daily life—not just for special occasions. And not always done up in elaborate arrangements. You don't always have to fuss. If you keep it simple, you'll be like-

lier to use flowers more often, more naturally. Sometimes the most pleasure-giving bouquet is nothing more than a bunch of daisies picked by a child.

To help you enjoy flowers in your home, I've listed some simple guidelines to remember:

- **COLOR**
- **SETTING**
- **SIZE**
- **SEASON**
- **SCENT**

COLOR, which I consider so very important, can help you achieve success most easily. It's usually the most obvious thing about a flower. Bright red poppies send one message, for example; sweet buttercups another. Choose flowers that coordinate with the room's color scheme, or that emphasize certain colors in it. And remember, color creates a mood.

When you don't have time to fuss, opt for a single-color bouquet that harmonizes with the room. The impact of the single color will usually be effective. I always love the look of white tulips in a big silver vase or overblown lilacs in an old blue-and-white pitcher.

Or, take the opposite approach: a

🦋 **OVERLEAF: A mantlepiece display of white freesias, lilacs, carnations, and tulips in antique glass vases.**

🦋 **OPPOSITE: A lovely room warmed by fabrics reflected in the leaves and flowers of a single, graceful bouquet.**

🐛 On my dressing table are blue glass vases filled with roses including Salet, Celsiana, Moss Rose, and Ispahan.

🐛 For a fragrance-filled morning, wake up to tulips and lilacs in a Victorian opaline cup set on a bedside table.

🐛 Corner tables in living rooms are fine for large arrangements like this one of foxglove, roses, and viburnum.

🐛 A small vase of my favorite flowers and cards in a toile fabric work box always brighten the top of my desk.

❧ Put a silver basket of violets on the bathroom sink and you'll smell the scent whenever you wash your face.

❧ I love flowers in the kitchen. Here, some hardy blue hydrangeas sit in a graceful, coordinated pottery vase.

❧ The perfect tea-tray, with tiny for-get-me-nots in an eighteenth-century tulip-shaped egg cup, sits on my bed.

❧ Even my closet has flowers in it! In this case, a full-blown antique velvet rose that decorates an Edwardian hat.

mixed-color bouquet with lots of colors, shapes, and textures in a simple, glass vase. The arrangement shines on its own.

The colors of flowers look different in artificial light than they do in natural light, so keep this in mind when selecting them for evening when lamps or candlelight will be used. Enhance the dramatic effect of an arrangement (especially if it's very large or very small) by illuminating it separately within the room.

SETTING is also key. Whether the decor of the room is formal, period, traditional, or very modern, the flowers should blend in comfortably and naturally. You don't want your flowers to be obtrusive.

In the eighteenth century, vases were designed as part of the decoration of a room and were never moved. Only the flowers changed. Nowadays, deciding where to place a vase of flowers is not always easy. Make a habit, as I have, of putting your arrangements where they will always look best. Choose a well-lit spot away from drafts and direct sunlight, where vases can't be easily knocked over.

SIZE is a factor. Consider the size of the flower-filled vase and its scale in relation to the room. Does it overwhelm the room or does it get lost? Either can be a problem. Practice working big *and* small.

I think some people are inclined to use too many flowers in one room. I would rather have one or two beautiful arrangements than lots of little ones spotted about the room, creating visual chaos.

SEASON often determines my choice of materials, as it does when I'm cooking, because I enjoy marking the passage of each with corresponding flowers and foliage, even though today almost anything is available out of season.

At Christmas, I like to try interesting

☙ ABOVE: Luxuriant roses on a hall table make a wonderful welcome for guests. The nineteenth-century bulb vases are made of hand-blown glass.
☙ OPPOSITE: A joyous display of summer sunflowers and delphinium buds sit in a jug in the kitchen.

combinations of evergreens, branches, and fruits. It's the best time to enjoy the results of last summer's flowers now dried in the form of potpourri and wreaths that I loved writing about in *The Scented Room*.

SCENT can affect our state of mind and is one of the reasons why we love having flowers around us. I like placing little bunches of scented flowers wherever their fragrance will be most appreciated. On a night table, for example. Or next to a favorite chair in the corner of a library or den. Constance Spry, in her book, *Flower Decoration,* calls these "intimate flowers," and I agree that small arrangements can sometimes be the most exquisite. The soothing effect of scent can be a blessing to someone who is ill or blind.

As with perfumes, what's pleasant to one person may seem overpowering to another. And like perfume, flower scents become more intense indoors. Remember that leaves also have a scent. See the fragrant lists that follow.

FRAGRANT FLOWERS

carnation	mignonette
freesia	mimosa
gardenia	mock orange
heliotrope	narcissus
honeysuckle	primrose
hyacinth	rose
jasmine	stock
lilac	sweet pea
lily	tuberose
lily-of-the-valley	violet, garden

FRAGRANT HERBS

bergamot	mint
costmary	rosemary
fennel	sage
hyssop	scented geraniums
lavender	southernwood
lemon balm	sweet woodruff
lemon verbena	thyme

FLOWERS ON

THE TABLE

We always feel welcome when, on entering a room, we find a display of flowers on the table. Where there are flowers about, the hostess appears glad, the children pleased, the very dog and cat grateful for our arrival, the whole scene and all the personages seem more hearty, homely, and beautiful. . . .

SHIRLEY HIBBERD,
Rustic Adornments for Homes of Taste,
1856

Flowers on the table have always been the natural companion to good food and good company. A beautiful table, set with flowers glowing among the candles, china, and crystal, sends an unspoken message of hospitality. In fact, that sentiment is conveyed by the flowers alone, even when the meal is a simple one served on everyday dishes.

Of all the preparations for a dinner party, setting and decorating the table is the task I most enjoy. The menu and flowers are planned in advance. Then, I start to assemble all the other elements on my kitchen counters—everything from vases and silver down to the last serving spoon —and I start having fun.

Aside from not constructing floral fortresses to protect guests from becoming too closely acquainted (this advice is from the English writer Beverley Nichols), there are no hard-and-fast rules for table decoration. And because of the temporary role or nature of the flowers, you can experiment more. Make the most of what you have. Dig into china closets.

Use your imagination. Get rid of preconceived ideas and take advantage of the myriad possibilities.

If you are having last-minute guests, you may bypass cut flowers altogether. Use a favorite potted plant—an idea that even Mrs. Beeton approved. In her *Book of Household Management,* that arbiter of Victorian taste, she writes: "plants suitable for the table may be employed, for they look in many cases as pretty as flowers." Slip your plant into an attractive china cachepot or tôle jardinière, add moss over the soil, and you're set.

The Victorians collected blossoms and floated them, tightly packed, in shallow dishes filled with water. Individual finger bowls are a variation of this idea. For these, I like using the flower heads or buds of buttercups, daisies, delphinium, lilies, roses, or orchids; the petals of roses or sweet peas; and well-shaped leaves like ivy or nasturtiums. This easy recipe

❧ **OVERLEAF: A few hours before guests arrive, all the table-setting elements are gathered together on my kitchen counter waiting for me to get started.**

❧ **OPPOSITE ABOVE: An abundant bouquet in an antique Sèvres vase takes center place on this lavish, flower-filled table set for a formal dinner.**

❧ **OPPOSITE BELOW: In close-up, an elegant finger bowl with floating miniatures of the roses, delphinium buds, and ivy used in the large arrangements.**

🌿 ABOVE: We often do not appreciate the beauty of green foliage. Here, rhubarb leaves make a nice centerpiece for lettuce-leaf dishes and paper-leaf coasters.

🌿 OPPOSITE: The ruby red of goblets and salad plates is echoed in a vivid lineup of assorted fruit and berries nicely accented with phlox bouquets at each place.

ले Sometimes the simplest solutions can be the most effective—left, a plant of
English ivy slipped into a porcelain cachepot, and, right, a rich, multicolor bouquet
of vivid French parrot tulips overflowing a very simple glass brandy snifter.

from my book, *A Bouquet of Flowers,*
makes six finger bowls.

ROSE FINGER BOWLS

1 cup scented rose petals
4 cups distilled water
6 drops rose oil
6 whole rose heads

1. Pick the rose petals in early morning.
Boil the water, and add the petals and oil.
2. Set aside until cool, then strain and discard the petals.
3. Fill finger bowls with the scented
water and one rose head. Place at each
setting when serving dessert.

It's also a nice idea to mix fresh flowers with other elements, such as ceramic,
sequined, or fresh fruits and vegetables.

To keep the blossoms watered, you'll
need to put them in little glass or plastic
tubes with rubber caps, called water piks.
Fill the vial with fresh water, insert the
stem through the hole in the cap, and
then place the flower in the centerpiece.
(And remember to re-fill the vials daily.)
This idea also comes in handy when including fresh flowers in wreaths, garlands, boutonnières or arrangements of
potted plants and found objects.

I also prefer to consider the season
when selecting table decoration. Seasonal
flowers, fruits, vegetables, and foliage not
only seem to me more appropriate, more
natural, but they also cost less. As I write
this at my kitchen table, for example, I'm
looking at eighteen of the yellowest,
freshest first daffodils of spring. Tonight
at dinner, this same bouquet will be the
cheery accompaniment to another sign of

Try mixing fresh flowers with other decorative pieces. Above is an arrangement of sequined fruit from the 1950s with real poppies and viburnum. To keep blossoms fresh, use water-filled vials like the one below, which holds a Gloriosa lily.

spring, fresh new asparagus! Every season has its special delights and we should get more in tune with nature, utilizing its bounty when it is offered in the garden and the shops. (For a list of my favorite flowers and foliage, see Chapter 5; for fruits and vegetables, Chapter 6.)

The subject of table decoration is a large one, but here, I'd like to highlight the key points:

- **COLOR**
- **SETTING**
- **SIZE**
- **LIGHT**
- **SCENT**

COLOR should be your guide in making all your table-setting elements work together. Before you start, make sure that the vases, linens, china, crystal, and accessories you will use color-coordinate with one another and let them dictate the colors of the flowers and foliage you choose.

SETTING, or the style of a room, should suggest a compatible choice of flowers. Is dinner going to be formal or relaxed? Will it be in the dining room or the kitchen? And as nowadays we sometimes use almost every part of the house for dining, whether it's a breakfast tray in the bedroom or a snack in the living room, it's always nice to include flowers.

SIZE means that the centerpiece should be in scale with the size of the table—neither too big, nor too small, and below or above eye level. There should be a balance between the flowers and the food and one should avoid the pretentious. I sometimes do a tall, full arrangement for the middle of the table, then remove it to the back of the buffet just before people are seated. In that case, I always make sure there are low individual flowers at each place. And remember, your flowers will be seen from all sides, from above, and at eye level, so they should look pretty from *every* angle.

LIGHT creates a mood and also affects the way we perceive color. This is espe-cially important to consider when arranging a table, because candles are often used. Certain colors, blue, for example, look washed out under artificial light. If you're planning an important meal, try in advance to see how the colors will look in the lighting you plan to use.

SCENT has long been a topic of debate when it comes to flowers for the table. I feel strongly about not using highly scented ones—like hyacinths or stocks—because, for some people, the scent interferes with their appreciation of the food.

And speaking of food, here's some for thought: why not try flowers in a soup, a salad, or on a dessert? We may think of this way of using flowers as fairly new, but actually it's an old custom. In the seventeenth century, the herbalist John Gerard wrote of the roses in England, where "children with delight make chains and pretty gewgawes of the fruit; and cookes and gentlewomen make tarts and such-like dishes for the pleasure thereof." In summer, I like using flowers in a salad of mixed greens with a simple dressing of wine vinegar and olive oil. Served on Staffordshire plates, it's as wonderful to look at as it is to eat.

Before using any flowers for food, you must first carefully identify them as edible and not poisonous or liable to cause an allergic reaction. Then sample them to be sure that you find them palatable. Some edible flowers I use are borage, chive blossoms, nasturtiums, pansies, roses, squash blossoms, and violets. Buy edible flowers on the day you'll be using them, or gather them from the garden early that morning. Wash them thoroughly, then gently blot them dry. Store everything—flower heads and petals—in a plastic bag in the refrigerator until you're ready to use them.

❧ OPPOSITE: **A glorious summer salad of mixed greens topped with the prettiest pansies and nasturtiums that I could find at our own farmer's market.**

SELECTING

EVERY LADY HER OWN

FLOWER GARDENER,

BY

LOUISA JOHNSON.

Vases

LONDON.

PUBLISHED BY Wm S ORR & Co PATERNOSTER ROW.
MDCCCLI.

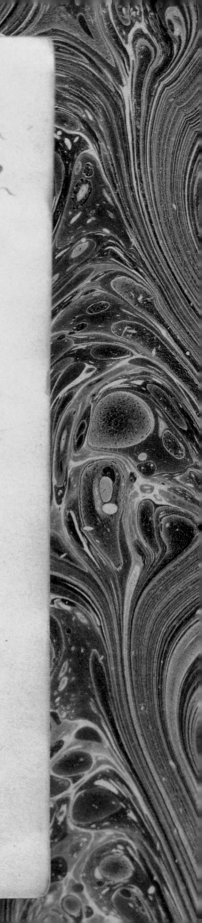

CHAPTER

The vase and the flowers, and the setting in which they'll be placed, are all dependent upon one another. A handful of flowers becomes something very different once you've put it into a vase—even if you've only fussed with it for a moment. And the kind of vase you use definitely alters the look of your flowers. So which comes first, the flowers or the vase? I approach it both ways, and you will, too. For example, one day I might need a suitable container for a bunch of spring flowers I impulsively purchased, while the next, the beauty of a newly acquired antique vase may inspire me to fill it with a special bouquet. The key is experimenting and becoming adept at using various approaches. And always keeping in mind that selecting a vase is as important as selecting your flowers.

I remember reading in an old book that a properly equipped flower room was a necessity. It's a dream I've always had. At the moment, however, my flower room is a cupboard in the butler's pantry off my kitchen, which holds the arranging tools and the containers I use for vases—all kinds, from my latest yard-sale find to a treasured silver vase in the shape of a basket—ready whenever I need them.

My collection has grown over the years, mostly with wonderful things I have found in antique shops, flea markets, craft shows, and at auction. Many were bargains, because sometimes what I consider to be an ideal container for flowers, others have ignored. Anything can be a vase as long as it holds water. I

like arranging flowers in pitchers—cream, milk, or large washbowl size, it doesn't matter. I place individual small bouquets in unmatched port glasses. Small slop bowls from old tea sets look elegant when filled with shrub roses or any full, short-stemmed flowers.

I'm always finding odd bits and pieces and adding them to my accumulation of containers. Many of them decorate the shelves and tables around our house and look almost as pretty without flowers as with them. So use your imagination. Look in your closets with a new eye. Check out the attic or basement when you go home to visit parents or relatives. Perhaps you'll find some other uses for the forgotten soup tureens, finger bowls, glasses, or wine coolers you may unearth.

Because I love antiques so much, I prefer using them whenever possible, though my cupboard holds a selection of classic, contemporary glass vases as well.

❧ OVERLEAF: An exquisite and practical book written in the middle nineteenth century for aspiring gardeners.
❧ OPPOSITE: An array of containers from the simplest to the most sophisticated (clockwise from top left): an old milk bottle and Queen Anne's lace; a recycled jelly jar blooming with roses; an antique pottery pipe stand sprouting dahlias, scabiosa, and snapdragons; and a trompe l'oeil tin urn for holding a single pink ranunculus.

&. **The delicate proportions and surfaces of the cut, pressed, and blown glass vases, above, make them graceful receptacles for flowers. OPPOSITE: A naive arrangement of sweet pansies in this little pressed glass basket from the 1930s.**

Some of these have small necks for simple bouquets. These serve as backup when the flowers I find at the florist or in the garden are too big, small, unwieldy, or otherwise inappropriate for my antique vases. In a pinch, these simple containers come in very handy.

The selection of vases is largely a matter of personal taste. Choosing a vase for your flowers is an important creative decision. Aesthetics plays a large role, but even so, you'll want to keep these three points in mind:

- **SIZE**
- **COLOR**
- **TYPES**

SIZE means that the container must be large enough to hold sufficient water, wide enough to hold the flowers comfortably at the neck and bottom, and high enough to accommodate the stems and keep the arrangement stable. The rule of thumb is that the bouquet should be one-and-a-half times the height of the vase, but my rule is to let the flowers themselves dictate the size of the arrangement.

COLOR can be a negative or a positive, depending on how you use it. If you have a ceramic vase decorated with multicolored patterns, or a colorful oriental ginger jar, for example, be sure that the colors of the flowers coordinate with it. If it works, this type of arrangement can be the prettiest you'll ever do. Of course, an easy solution is to use clear glass vases or other neutral-color receptacles.

🐚 ABOVE: The gleam of silver: left to right, in an embossed pitcher, rose bowl, trumpet vase, English trophy cup, pillar vase, small basket, and assorted bud vases. BELOW: Old-fashioned lilacs, my mother's favorite flowers, and mine too.

TYPES of containers can be anything from cut glass, to straw baskets, to hammered brass, and everything in between. But whatever type you choose, it should be compatible with the flowers. For instance, I think summer flowers look enchanting in country baskets. So consider whether the flowers are grand or simple, dainty or sturdy, and then decide which type of vase is most suitable for the effect you wish to create:

Glass—Blown, pressed, cut, or colored glass vases, either old or modern, are ideal for almost anything, especially for elegant arrangements of flowering branches and foliage. I also like all white flowers in clear glass vases. Remember that the stems will show and become an important part of the composition, so

🌾 ABOVE: Colorful patterns on ceramic containers of various shapes and sizes, including tubs, urns, bowls, pitchers, and cups. BELOW: An antique blue Wedgwood rose bowl, the ideal place for a dainty bouquet of perfect Iceberg roses.

your glass vases must always be kept perfectly clean to look their best. Avoid using milky stemmed flowers that will discolor or cloud the water.

Metal—Choices in metal include new and antique silver vases (gracefully elegant against dark wood), and brass, copper, pewter, bronze, or cast-iron containers, which come in a wide variety of shapes and sizes. In silver baskets and vases, I like old-fashioned flowers like peonies, lilacs, and roses; in hammered metal bowls and urns, I often use grasses, seed pods, and bunches of foliage.

Ceramics—Porcelain, pottery, and terra-cotta containers, which come in lovely shapes from wall pockets to cornucopias, are fun to use because they're so ornamental. Be careful to select a pat-

🐦 For simpler, more informal arrangements, the best containers are often rustic baskets, trugs, and terra-cotta pots like the ones above. BELOW: A Victorian basket of gilded straw holding a big frothy spring bouquet of perfumed bridal wreath.

tern and color compatible with your flowers. I find ceramic vases ideal for multicolor summer bouquets of zinnias, ranunculus, hollyhocks, snapdragons, calendulas, cornflowers, and sweet peas.

Baskets—From homespun weaves to the most intricate lacquered or ethnic works of art, baskets have a natural affinity with flowers because they're made from growing things. I like to use them with colorful wildflowers, or shrub flowers like bridal wreath, forsythia, and magnolia. Baskets also look fresh lined with large leaves like rhubarb or grape leaves and filled with fruits and vegetables.

Wood, Marble, Alabaster—These materials often can be found in sophisticated shapes like urns and jardinières, tin-lined and originally meant for

Ã‰🐚 ABOVE: **Classic ornamental shapes, including, left to right, an art nouveau brass vase, a wire basket, a wood and glass bud vase, a copper bowl, and, between two cast-iron urns, a similar double-tiered vase, below, hold roses and viburnum.**

potted plants. For these containers, I especially like deep vibrant flowers, such as red roses or purple hyacinths.

There are also other things to think about concerning your containers:

First, all porous receptacles, such as baskets or those made of wood or unglazed terra-cotta, must be lined in order to hold water. Some people have tin liners custom made. I find it handy to use glass jars, recycled plastic containers, or, if a basket is shallow, aluminum pie tins.

Finally, always be sure to put your containers away absolutely clean and dry. A poorly cleaned vase can harbor and foster the growth of bacteria, shortening the life of your flowers. So after using, rinse each vase with a little household bleach and then dry it thoroughly.

PREPARING

FLOWERS

In *An Island Garden,* Celia Thaxter charmingly describes how, in the very early morning, she collected the flowers she would later arrange in thirty vases for the family hotel on Appledore Island. After carefully picking each bloom, she quickly dropped it into water. "Gathered in this way," she explains, "they have no opportunity to lose their freshness, indeed, the exquisite creatures hardly know they have been gathered at all."

Even though this was written in 1894, it still serves as a good reminder that the flowers we cut or buy are living things that must be properly prepared and fed before they're arranged so they'll stay fresh and beautiful for as long as possible. In this chapter I've included a number of tips that I hope will help you to do this in a sensible, organized way.

First, however, consider which botanicals you want to use to create the best possible arrangements. To help you decide, the following list offers suggestions for flowers, including my favorite perennials, annuals, and bulbs; graceful flowering branches, shrubs, and vines; and various foliage and grasses that I've chosen for their interesting shapes and tones.

Whether you purchase or grow your

✷ OVERLEAF: **Tulips, ranunculus, roses, and foliage are conditioned in deep cool water before being arranged.**

✷ OPPOSITE: **My niece fills galvanized buckets with water so that the fresh flowers she has gathered from our garden can be immediately immersed.**

own flowers, be sure to look in the Source Directory in the back of this book. It includes a list of florists where you can buy cut flowers. And places where you can order seedlings, seeds, and bulbs if you are fortunate to have your own garden and can plant whatever you choose. Then you are ready to start!

 FLOWERS

ageratum	daffodil
allium	dahlia
astroemeria	daisy
anemone	delphinium
aster	euphorbia
astilbe	feverfew
auricula	flax
baby's breath	flowering tobacco
bee balm	forget-me-not
bellflower	foxglove
bells of Ireland	freesia
bleeding heart	fritillaria
bluebell	fuchsia
bouvardia	gentian
calendula	gerbera
candytuft	gladiolus
Canterbury bell	grape hyacinth
carnation	heather
chrysanthemum	heliotrope
clematis	hollyhock
cleome	hyacinth
columbine	iris
coreopsis	jonquil
cornflower	lady's mantle
cosmos	larkspur
coxcomb	lavender
crocus	liatris

FLOWERS (continued)

lily
lily-of-the-valley
lisianthus
loosestrife
love-in-a-mist
lupine
marigold
monkshood
morning glory
narcissus
nasturtium
orchid
pansy
peony
petunia
phlox
pinks
polyanthus
poppy
primrose
Queen Anne's lace
ranunculus
rose

rudbeckia
salvia
scabiosa
scented geranium
sedum
snapdragon
Solomon's seal
statice
stock
sunflower
sweet alyssum
sweet pea
sweet rocket
sweet William
tansy
teasel
tuberose
tulip
veronica
violet
waxflower
yarrow
zinnia

FLOWERING BRANCHES, SHRUBS, AND VINES

almond
azalea
bridal wreath
butterfly bush
clematis
crab apple
crepe myrtle
dogwood
flowering cherry
flowering quince
forsythia

gardenia
honeysuckle
hydrangea
laburnum
lilac
magnolia
mock orange
mountain laurel
orange blossom
peach
pear

FLOWERING BRANCHES, SHRUBS, AND VINES
(continued)

plum
pussy willow
rhododendron

rose-of-Sharon
viburnum
wisteria

FOLIAGE

artemesia
barberry
bay
beech
begonia
bergenia
box
costmary
eucalyptus
euonymous
ferns
galax leaf
garden euphorbia
grape vine
hemlock
holly
hosta
ivy
juniper

lamb's ear
laurel
lemon leaf
parsley
periwinkle
pine
pittosporum
privet
rhododendron
rhubarb
rue
sage
santolina
Scotch broom
sedum
Solomon's seal
spruce
tree peony
violet

GRASSES

beargrass
Bowles' golden grass
cloud grass

hare's tail grass
oat grass
quaking grass

🌾 The entrance to our cutting garden with a bright summer display of delphinium, cosmos, and climbing roses.

🌾 Me, taking a gardening break in the cool shade of the arbor that will supply us with Concord grapes in autumn.

 ## Gathering Flowers

Beverley Nichols said of Gertrude Jekyll, "Not only did she 'arrange' her flowers but she grew them, and when she carried them indoors, her fingers were muddy." And in her book, *Flower Decoration,* Ms. Jekyll reminds us that "when new gardens are planned the reserve gardens should not be forgotten."

The advantage of a cutting or reserve garden is that it allows you to happily gather all the flowers you want without depleting your borders or landscaping. I think a cutting garden is one of the most rewarding gardens you can plant. Even a small one will provide you with a steady supply of flowers and foliage.

Our cutting garden is located across from the vegetable garden on a north-south axis to ensure maximum sunlight. It's not large, about twelve feet by twenty, and is framed by a picket fence that we found many years ago in an antiques shop. (I later discovered that most colonial gardens were surrounded by picket fences to keep animals out, the points at top discouraging roosting fowls!) The entrance is a trellis built by my father, and

in the center of the garden is a sundial. Old-fashioned roses, clematis, and morning glories climb over everything.

The garden is filled with many types of my favorite perennials, annuals, and bulbs. Some are the old varieties, many of which are more hardy and require less watering than the newer kinds.

If you have a cutting garden, here are some tips for gathering flowers:

• The best time to cut flowers is in the early morning or early evening, when their scent is strongest and moisture retention is greatest. Flowers go limp if picked during the hottest hours of the day. In fact, Constance Spry suggests cutting them the day before they're needed, allowing the flowers a long drink. When deciding what to cut, pay attention to . . .

Flower Heads—Choose blossoms that have a firm, crisp feel and are in various stages of opening, also some buds.

Stems and Foliage—Look for stems that are strong and straight, bearing healthy foliage. I always cut the stems as long as possible. (I will probably shorten them later, but I leave my options open.) Always cut stems on an angle to maximize the surface that absorbs water. The best

🐝 Flowering branches of bridal wreath, cherry or magnolia—or frothy crab apple, shown here—make naturally graceful additions to most flower arrangements.

cutting tools are a sharp knife, or florist shears that will cut the stems cleanly. Don't tear at the flowers by using scissors. They'll pinch the stems closed.

• Never cut botanicals and leave them to be picked up later. The quicker you put your flowers into water after cutting them, the longer they will last.

• Take some plastic or metal buckets or pitchers down to the garden, fill them to the neck with water, and place them in a shady spot, ready to receive the flowers *immediately* after they've been cut. Leave room in the containers; stems expand as they take in water, and overcrowding could crush them.

Buying Flowers

If you are going to buy your flowers, whether from a florist or a corner market, here are some things to keep in mind:

• All of us have purchased flowers that have died prematurely or just didn't do well. In many cases, this is because they had not been properly conditioned before you bought them. Buy your flowers from a reliable florist or market, and examine them carefully. The healthiest flowers are the ones that will last the longest. Here's what to look for:

Flower Heads—Blossoms should have a firm, crisp look, the heads shouldn't droop, and the petals shouldn't be bruised. Look at the center and if the pollen has built up, the flower won't last long after you get it home. And look for buds at different stages of opening so that they won't flower all at once.

Foliage—The leaves on the stems should be strong and healthy, not wilted, bruised, or discolored. Healthy foliage indicates a healthy flower.

Stems—Stems should be strong.

🐚 Hammer woody stems like lilac, crab apple, and Chinese redbuds, above, before placing in water, below right. Scrape thick stems, like Bradford pear, below left.

 howto ABOVE: When choosing flowers, look for signs of health
and freshness. The stem of the white tulip, left, for example, looks spongy and old, while the stem of the pink
parrot tulip next to it is a fresh green. The foliage of the
first snapdragon looks limp—a sign of age. Even though
the leaves will be removed, they should always look fresh.

howto RIGHT: A clear geometric glass vase that was lined
with bear grass stems, then filled with graceful orchids.

🌸 **ABOVE:** All flower stems should be cut on a slant, as shown here, left to right, on the bells of Ireland and gerbera. Woody stems like those of the wax flower, viburnum, and pussy willow, shown next, are cut, then scraped and hammered or slit at the tips. This allows the stems to take in a lot more water, enabling the flowers to last longer.

🌸 **RIGHT:** Elegant lily stems become a graceful part of the design when turned on the bias in a clear glass vase.

❦ Here are two techniques that can be used to condition or revive flowers before they've been arranged. The stems of the roses above have been cut at the tips, tightly wrapped in newspaper, then placed in cold water to stand overnight. The amaryllis is waiting for water to be gently poured down into its hollow stem.

❦ OPPOSITE: The stems of colorful flowers are cut short to fit a small glass vase.

Check the ends to make sure they're not discolored, spongy, or torn.

• When bringing flowers home, make sure you keep them protected from extremes of heat or cold. In fact, it's a good idea to make the flower shop the last stop on your list so the flowers won't have a chance to wilt. I always keep a bucket and paper towels in my car. When I buy flowers, I wrap wet paper towels around the stems and pop the flowers into the bucket for the drive home.

 ## Conditioning Flowers to Make Them Last

Cut flowers *must* be prepared before they are arranged. Many people tend to skip this step and just put their flowers directly into a vase. This may be the easy way, but it is not the right way. It's vital that you do everything to ensure that your flowers keep fresh for as long as possible and that means conditioning them as *soon* as you get them home.

Before you begin, choose a place where you can work without making too much of a mess. This could be a potting shed, garage, or any area with access to water and a work surface for your flowers, containers, and tools. A kitchen counter will do, too. I lay newspapers down to contain the resulting chaos and make the cleanup less time consuming.

Important points to consider when conditioning flowers are:

- **WATER**
- **FOLIAGE**
- **STEMS**

WATER is essential. The moment you bring your flowers into the house, put them in the deepest container of water, for as long as possible. (Several hours at least for store-bought, or, as I mentioned before, even overnight for ones from the garden.) Remember always to use tepid or warm water, which the stems will absorb more quickly than ice cold water.

Then place the container in a cool spot that's free from drafts—a garage or basement with a cement or stone floor is ideal—and let the flowers take a nice long drink before you work with them.

FOLIAGE that is submerged in water will quickly rot, encouraging the growth of bacteria, which can kill flowers and foul the water in the vase. To avoid this, remove all leaves and side shoots that you think will stand below the water line. (If you are using roses, this is a good time to remove thorns with a sharp knife.)

You might prefer to remove all leaves from the stems and save the pretty ones to use later in the arrangement. Or you can leave the foliage on the upper part of the stems (especially if using lilacs or roses for example) for a more natural look. Remember, if you're using a glass vase, the stems will be visible so make sure they're neatly shorn without bits of debris and foliage clinging to them.

STEMS need to be conditioned in various ways before you start your arrangement. There are different methods for different types of botanicals, but they all have one common purpose: to enable the flower to take in as much water as possible.

🐝 **To wire a flower, gently push a piece of wire into the base of the blossom. Take a second wire twice as long as the first and insert it across the base.**

🐝 **Keeping one end of the second wire longer than the other, fold the three ends together and wrap them tightly with floral tape, tapering from the top.**

After you've dealt with foliage and thorns, cut the tips of all the stems, *again, under water*. This eliminates any air bubbles that formed within the stems when they were first cut. Re-cutting is important because these bubbles prevent water from flowing up the stem, ultimately shortening the life of the flower. To re-cut, simply fill a sink with tepid water and, holding each stem under water, cut ¼ to ½ inch off on a slant.

After re-cutting, most flowers are ready to be arranged. There are some exceptions that need additional attention:

You can treat botanicals with hard *woody stems*—forsythia, lilac, and magnolia, for example—by crushing or splitting the ends. Gently hammer the tips, or make a two-inch vertical cut up the base of each stem with sharp shears. You can also scrape the bark with a sharp knife several inches from the bottom.

Botanicals with stems that contain *milky sap* need special treatment. For in-stance, all euphorbias, poppies, and hollyhocks will last longer if you cauterize the end of the stem by holding it over a candle or match until it turns black. This prevents the sap from solidifying at the tip and blocking the intake of water.

Hollow-stemmed flowers such as amaryllis, delphinium, and lupine can be upended, filled with water, and plugged with a piece of cotton wool. Hold your thumb over the end to prevent the cotton or water from escaping as you place each stem into the water-filled vase.

Tips for Reviving Flowers

Flowers can wilt either *before* or *after* you have arranged them. If this occurs, here are some suggestions:

• Some tired-looking flowers can be revived by entirely immersing them in cool water for up to 15 minutes until crisp. Or you can mist the blossoms and leaves, which also absorb moisture. Ca-

 Wire-stemmed flowers are used in bouquets like this one of ranunculus and roses with green viburnum and ivy, and streamers of shiny satin ribbon.

mellias, gardenias, orchids, roses, and violets respond well to this.

• If only the flower head is droopy, prick the stem directly under it with a straight pin. This will release trapped air and allow water to be absorbed without obstruction. Roses, ranunculus, tulips, and zinnias respond to this treatment.

• Sometimes the blossoms and stems of certain tall flowers become limp. If this occurs, re-cut the ends, then roll the flowers in newspaper. Let them stand overnight in a bucket filled with cold water up to their necks. Roses, tulips, and zinnias are often revived by this method.

• Some wilting flowers can be revived with boiling hot water. Simply re-cut the stems, place in a container filled with several inches of hot water, and let them sit for a minute (or as long as it takes for them to perk up). This eliminates any air bubbles in the stems, enabling them to absorb the cooler vase water more quickly. Many flowers re-

spond to this, especially astilbe, chrysanthemums, dahlias, delphinium, foxglove, hollyhocks, hydrangeas, lilacs, and roses.

• Frequent re-cutting of the ends of fleshy stemmed flowers will help prolong their life. Daffodils, hyacinths, irises, and tulips are aided by this practice.

Wiring Flower Stems

Wiring is the substitution of a wire for the original stem of a flower, and it must be done before starting an arrangement. This technique is often used for flowers that are going to be made into wedding bouquets, boutonnières, and garlands. The photographs above offer simple instructions, featuring an exquisite bouquet by Rita Bobry of Spring St. Garden in New York City.

Wiring is also used to strengthen or support a weak-stemmed flower, or to help it keep its shape in an arrangement. This is done simply by inserting a long piece of wire lengthwise through the center of the stem up to the base of the flower head. Some hard-stemmed flowers, however, must be wired on the outside by twisting the wire gently and neatly around the stem from top to bottom.

All of these techniques allow for more flexibility than the natural stems provide, so that you can twist or bend flowers more easily and gracefully.

You can use florist wire for small as well as large flowers, as it comes in many thicknesses. Always use the finest gauge possible, so that it is not obvious. Wiring is not for every flower. Some won't survive for prolonged periods once you've removed the stem.

Flowers that are frequently wired include: camellia, carnation, chrysanthemum, daisy, daffodil, delphinium bud, freesia, gardenia, hyacinth bud, orchid, ranunculus, rose, and tulip.

Now that your flowers have been conditioned, they're ready to be arranged. The next chapter will tell you how to do this in simple yet beautiful ways.

ARRANGING
FRUITS, AND

Flowers, Vegetables

CHAPTER 6

Much has been written on the subject of arranging flowers, with advice ranging from the "don't fuss" philosophy to the "flower arranging is Art" school of thought. My own approach falls somewhere between the two. That is, I consider flower arranging an art, a form of creative self-expression. But if you take yourself too seriously, you'll never have any fun—and probably won't produce anything very satisfactory as a result.

Really *look* at the colors, shapes, and textures of your flowers to appreciate the unique characteristics of each. As you work with the flowers, let them guide and inspire you. You will work more spontaneously this way.

Of course, there are certain basics to be mastered—guidelines that will become second nature, once you've absorbed them, enabling you to express yourself freely and work intuitively.

After looking at one of Vincent van Gogh's paintings, his physician, Dr. Gachet, remarked, "How difficult it is to be simple." Indeed, it is, even with flowers. But I think that, ultimately, with a simple, common-sense approach you can avoid the overstudied and always create something charming and tasteful, whether you prefer delicate little bouquets or large, flamboyant ones. Here are some points to consider before you start:

- **COLOR**
- **TEXTURE**
- **PROPORTION**
- **BALANCE**
- **SHAPE**

COLOR should be your first consideration. Rather than the type of flower, it is the *color* of the flower that is most important. If the colors are in harmony with one another, your bouquets will be pleasing to the eye. When in doubt, or pressed for time, use a mass of only one type of flower in one color: all yellow tulips, all white lilies, and so on. The impact of the pure color carries the day.

You can take this idea one step further by using monochromatic colors. Gertrude Jekyll explains in *Home and Garden:* "One might prepare a range of at least thirty tints . . . all of which might be called pink." An example might be a bouquet of peonies from palest pink to deep rose. Or assorted flowers in cool shades of blues to purples.

Another approach is to mix a single color with green—either leaves, or green flowers such as bells of Ireland, green tulips, or viburnum. As garden writer Louise Beebe Wilder says in her book, *Color in My Garden,* "It is said that green is the last color to be appreciated even by the most aesthetic. . . ." And I agree.

Leaves have a quiet dignity by themselves. Even in the middle of summer, with a whole range of flowers available, I

OVERLEAF: Bunches of daisies, roses, and sweet peas ready to be arranged.

OPPOSITE: An offering of parsley is a sign of good-will. Here, it is in a silver beaker with elegant blue and white Chinese jars brimming with peonies.

🐚 ABOVE: The simplicity of a mass of all white flowers in a vase always looks elegant and stately and suits any room. Pictured here, giant amaryllis, a luminous piece of crystal, and silver.

🐚 BELOW: A monochromatic arrangement using one type of flower—in this case, sweet peas in varying shades of the same color. A green ceramic vase is a perfect complement to a froth of pink.

think it's fun to go to the garden and pick a big bunch of rhubarb leaves to arrange in a vase. And don't forget, there are also yellow, maroon, gray, and even variegated leaves, making them another good color source. Whatever you use, remember that leaves aren't just an accessory but an integral part of the composition. (For suggestions, see Chapter 5.)

Sometimes, the nicest kind of flower arrangement is the multicolor bouquet, using as many different flowers in as many colors as possible. I love to gather a sampling of whatever is in bloom at the moment—the exuberance of color becomes a statement in itself. You can also try a more sophisticated palette using colors that blend or (more difficult) contrast with one another but still work together.

Color is a very personal thing. And while some people have a wonderful eye for combining colors, and others have no color sense at all, nearly everyone has a favorite color. Consider your own preferences. Study the relationship between one color and another. Have fun experimenting with new combinations!

TEXTURE is another consideration in arranging flowers, and one that's often ignored. Look at the flowers and leaves you want to use. Are their surfaces smooth or rough? Shiny or dull? All these factors will visually affect the look of your finished arrangement (as will the surface texture of your vase). Experiment by combining leaves and flowers of various textures to see how they relate to one another.

PROPORTION is the happy relationship between the vase and the flowers. As I mentioned previously, the rule of thumb is that the height of the flowers be one-and-a-half times the height of the vase. There are many exceptions to this rule—times when you'll want your flowers to overshadow the vase, or the opposite. Working out pleasing proportions will become second nature to you if you keep in mind an imaginary point above the vase that will mark the finished height.

For example, you can decide to do a low design with all short-stemmed flowers or a tall one using only long stems. Or a dramatic combination of both in one large vase, as shown in the photograph on page 69, taken at La Grenouille, one of the most beautiful restaurants in New York City. Charles Masson, Jr., carries on his father's tradition of filling the restaurant with ten very grand and thirty smaller lavish bouquets that fill every corner of this enchanted spot. Each is an example of a masterly eye for proportion.

Some people are afraid to cut the long stems of flowers. There's nothing wrong with doing this, and *not* doing it can sometimes limit your possibilities. Long stems give you the option of flexibility—if you need the height, you have it. But when their length makes them too difficult to handle, or inappropriate for the vase you have in mind, by all means, cut them. In many cases, doing so will make the flowers look dramatically different. Some flowers such as roses are priced by the length of the stem, so if you plan ahead, you can save money.

❧ ABOVE: Another approach is to use flowers of just one color with a variety of green botanicals. The example shown includes green bells of Ireland, Queen Anne's lace, and viburnum, with peach-hued tulips, roses, and gerbera.

❧ BELOW: Try the unexpected—like this multicolor bouquet of miniature hollyhocks, andromeda, roses, and sweet peas that looks fresh from the garden.

BALANCE refers to the comfortable relationship of all the elements in the arrangement. A balanced composition should look visually "stable" when finished, with an equal distribution of weight. This doesn't mean that the arrangement must be symmetrical, just counterbalanced. All the elements should flow with a visual rhythm that draws the eye through the arrangement in the same way the viewer's eye is drawn through a well-composed painting. A repetition of a certain color, shape, or texture can establish or alter the rhythm.

An arrangement that is top-heavy in the vase will be off balance and could fall over. Keep an eye on the height of your flowers and make sure that the vase is filled with marbles or pebbles to provide extra weight at the bottom, if necessary.

SHAPE is very important. Will your arrangement be tall and loosely filled with flowers or will it be small and tightly packed? Remember, as Julia Berral, the noted flower arranger, once said, "Flowers should have nodding room." Even if you are intentionally massing them, avoid crowding your flowers. You should be able to see the form of each flower head. And of course, you can appreciate the flower in all its minute detail by using just one simple blossom in a vase.

Think about how your flowers will be seen. Will they be viewed from all sides or be positioned flat against a wall? Will they be seen at eye level or from above? This should be determined well in advance, so that you can work in the round, as a sculptor does, or save time by concentrating on just the front.

Then consider the general outline or silhouette of the arrangement you want to make. If I'm working with a large vase, I usually envision a triangle or a fan

🌿 Use flowers with short or long stems—or a mix of both, depending upon your vase. The ranunculus, above left, were used as cut from the garden, while the flowers at right were cut very short to fit in an unusual bud vase.
🌿 OPPOSITE: Elegant flowers of many lengths at La Grenouille in New York.

🌿 Groups of many blossoms like these, above, all picked in my garden on one day in August, look wonderful. Each is in a different vase, all collected at antique shows and flea markets over the years. Below, you can use multiples of the same vase to highlight ordinary kinds of flowers—for example, these carnations.

shape. With small vases, I keep a circle or oval shape in mind. It's a method that generally works well for me.

When you actually begin filling the vase, you have some options. Some people start in the center and work out. Others create an outline, putting the tallest flowers in first. Still another method, one I use a lot, is to insert the largest masses first, creating a background into which all the other flowers will be placed.

Make sure that the flowers are recessed at different heights to create a feeling of depth. Strive for something that has dimension. Your composition should also look as natural as possible, not stiff, so the flower heads should not all be facing in the same direction. Observe how the flowers grow in nature.

People often ask how they can better judge whether they have enough flowers for their arrangements. I always make certain to have more flowers than I think I'll need. This gives me extra choices and allows me to make my compositions as full and abundant as I like. A skimpy vase of flowers can be very unappealing. An overflowing one, on the other hand, is usually very effective. If I have flowers left over, it gives me the perfect excuse to fill the house with little bud vases.

Supplies You Will Need for Arranging

Before arranging your flowers, make sure that you have the correct tools and equipment on hand. Today, the choice can be bewildering, so you must be as educated as possible about what you will—or won't—need. Here's the list:

CUTTING TOOLS come in such a wide variety that the choices can be confusing, but I use three basic tools:

A folding knife is indispensable and very important for scraping stems and cutting blocks of foam.

Always consider where you'll be putting your arrangement before you start. This country bouquet—viewed from the front, above, and the back, below—was designed to serve as a centerpiece for an informal dinner, so it had to look perfect from every angle. The colorful assortment of flowers including peonies, roses, lilacs, ranunculus, grape hyacinth, sweet peas, ageratum, and cornflowers were cut short and arranged in a block of green floral foam within the wood crate, giving them a lovely natural feeling.

🌾 Four simple-to-follow steps for making a round-shaped composition. ABOVE LEFT: Start with a mass of full flowers, like hydrangea, to establish the framework and shape of the arrangement. Then, above right, add dahlias, cockscomb, and sedum, positioning them so that the color is balanced and not all bunched in one spot.

🌾 ABOVE LEFT: To give this composition a sense of movement and depth, finish it with lacy lady's mantle and graceful amaranthus. The bouquet pictured above right is a variation. In this arrangement, all the sprigs of the same flowers are first tied together in small bunches and then inserted to make arranging the flowers easier.

Florist or garden scissors are a must and can be used for cutting almost everything. Do not use all-purpose scissors.

Pruning shears of good quality are essential for snipping off thick or woody branches or stems.

FLOWER HOLDERS help position and support flowers in their container. Sometimes you need them, sometimes not. If I'm doing a casual arrangement, I simply arrange the flowers in my hand, working quickly while adding more to the bunch. Then I trim the stems, let the flowers settle naturally in the vase, and fuss with them a bit to get the look I want.

If I have more time, I arrange the flowers by placing them in the vase one by one, criss-crossing the stems. Woven together this way, the stems support each other and eliminate the need for a flower holder. This method is nice when using a glass vase where the stems show. At other times, I use the following:

Flexible chicken wire is useful for positioning large masses of flowers or formal arrangements in containers, especially baskets and wide-mouthed vases. To work with it, fold a narrow length into an accordion shape, or crumple it lightly into a ball, then push it carefully into the container. When released, it will press snugly into place against the sides, ready to gently receive the flower stems. If it isn't stable enough, you can always tape it to the vase with waterproof floral tape. A flat piece of chicken wire can also be fit like a grid across the mouth of a glass vase, taped into place, and camouflaged with sphagnum moss after the flowers have been arranged.

Floral foam is ideal in shallow containers for short-stemmed flowers or flower heads. It's also a good support for masses of flowers and twigs, or when you want your flowers to drape over the sides of the vase at different angles.

Floral foam comes in two different forms: the green, porous type (called Oasis), which is water absorbent and used for fresh flower arrangements; and the brown, nonabsorbent type (Sahara), used for dried flower arrangements. Available in a variety of sizes, the brick shape is the most common.

Oasis is light and very easy to handle. Just cut it to the shape you want, submerge it thoroughly in water, until no bubbles come to the surface, then wedge into the container. Even though the foam is pre-soaked before use, the container in which you place it should always be filled with water. Otherwise, the foam becomes dry and can suck moisture from the flowers. If you are using an especially large block of floral foam, you can wrap it with chicken wire to prevent it from crumbling, and secure it in the container with criss-crossed pieces of waterproof adhesive tape or anchor pins.

Do not insert your flowers into floral foam by pushing on the blossoms, or you might break the stems. Instead, hold the bottom of the stems to insert them.

Pin holders are sharp, pinlike spikes set into a heavy lead base (which also helps to weight the vase). They're used in Ikebana (the art of Japanese flower arranging) to stabilize flowers in flat, shallow dishes, or in very simple line arrangements using just a few flowers. Hairpin holders, a variation, have more flexible spikes and can be used to hold flowers at any angle. Glass frogs and metal mesh holders are like pin holders except that they have holes in them for receiving the tips of stems.

Marbles and polished pebbles are designed especially for stabilizing flowers in a glass vase where other holders would be visible and possibly unattractive. They can also be used to camouflage a pin holder placed in the base of a glass vase.

FLORAL ACCESSORIES complete your collection of necessary equipment. You will need several of the following items:

Floral tape is a must for wrapping the stems of bouquets or wired flowers. You wind it around the stem of the

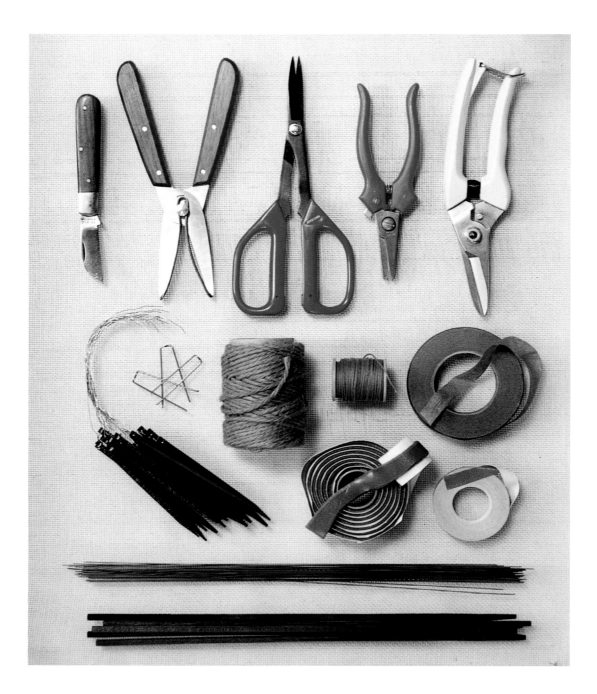

❧ You may not need all of the flower-arranging tools and accessories shown here, but it's always nice to know what's what. Reading from left to right, they include, top row: a folding knife, florist shears, garden scissors, and small and large pruning shears. Second row: floral pins, green twine, a spool of florist wire, and a roll of floral tape. Third row: flower picks with attached wire, and rolls of floral adhesive and waterproof tape. Bottom rows: various thicknesses of floral wire.

ᑐ The wide variety of flower holders available, left to right, top row: A brown floral-foam brick for dry arrangements, and a green one for fresh. Between them are anchor pins, and on the far right, crumpled chicken wire. Second row: Two metal mesh flower holders flanking a large pin holder with a heavy lead base. Third row: Two plastic water pics, a small pin holder, and a small hairpin holder. Bottom row: Amber and clear glass frogs, clear marbles, and a large hairpin holder.

❧ ABOVE: When working with fruits and vegetables just about anything can be used to compose a beautiful picture. This is our Victorian mantel, which I decorated for Thanksgiving last year. First, I went to the farmer's market for wonderful seasonal produce, like varnished gourds in various colors and baby pumpkins. Then, from our garden I gathered dried Chinese lanterns, bittersweet branches, and lots of colorful leaves. I used a stand of wrapped wheat, center, as a focal point.

❧ LEFT: A lush idea for decorating a sideboard or a table in the foyer when flowers are not available: compose a clever arrangement of ornamental kale, apples, grapes, pears, limes, tangerines, and an eggplant on a big tray.

flower, overlapping and stretching it as you work downward, then pinch it with your fingers at the tip to finish.

Waterproof tape, a sticky green adhesive tape, is used to anchor foam, chicken wire, or other flower holders to the base or sides of the container.

Florist wire comes in straight pieces or on a reel in a variety of thicknesses. It's essential for wiring flowers and also is used for securing foam or chicken wire to the insides of baskets.

Floral adhesive is a sticky clay that comes on a roll. It can be used to stick flower holders or anchor pins to the bottom of a vase or any other container.

Anchor pins are plastic pieces with prongs, used to support a large block of floral foam when attached with floral adhesive to the bottom of a container.

Flower picks are thin spikes of green wood that come with or without wire attached to the top. Picks are commonly used to secure fruits, vegetables, and flowers to floral foam or to each other.

Water picks are plastic vials that hold flower stems in water. They are discussed in detail in Chapter 3.

String, in shades of green, is always handy to have, especially for tying bunches of flowers together when you are fashioning bouquets.

Almost as important as how you arrange your flowers is how you care for them afterward. Flowers are living things that should not be neglected. They will have drunk the most water the day after you arranged them, especially if you used absorbent floral foam. Check the water level daily or whenever you walk by your flowers, and, if necessary, refill the vase up to the top with cool tap water.

It isn't necessary to take the flowers out of the vase to replace the water. Flowers can suffer from overhandling, which will negate all your hard work. You can stand the vase in a sink without removing the flowers, letting the water run into the vase until the old water has been flushed out. This is convenient if the water has a foul odor or if you have a clear glass vase in which the water has become murky.

Flowers will last longer in a humid setting, so it helps in hot weather to spray the leaves and blossoms because, like the stems, they absorb water. A humidifier will also help in a very dry room.

Here are some simple tips for keeping the water and flowers in your vases as fresh as possible:

• A commercial flower food or preservative added to the water will make the flowers last longer. (Check first if using these products in a glass vase, as some of them color the water.)

• To neutralize stagnant odors or murky water, add household bleach (from several drops to a teaspoonful for a medium to large vase). This will kill the bacteria and freshen the water.

• A piece of naturally absorbent charcoal added to the vase can clear up cloudy water and sweeten bad odors.

• Adding an aspirin to the water retards bacterial growth and encourages the leaf pores to close, thereby limiting moisture loss.

• Some people add a little sugar or lemonade to the water. Sucrose seems to have a good effect on flowers, helping move moisture through the stems.

Some people believe that an old penny in the vase helps the flowers live longer! However, there is no substitute for always cleaning your containers with a little bleach and drying them thoroughly after using them, as discussed in Chapter 4. This, more than anything, will help extend the life of your flowers.

Cold works too. I sometimes do a flower arrangement a day in advance and refrigerate it overnight. I even do the same with cut flowers. This guarantees my having perky flowers the next day.

And finally, when the flowers do begin to fade, I discard the wilted ones then re-cut the stems of the remaining flowers, and rearrange them. Sometimes, I add full flowers like Queen Anne's lace,

FRUITS AND VEGETABLES

RED

apple
currant
grape
peach
pepper, red
plum
pomegranate
radish
raspberry
strawberry
tomato

ORANGE

gourd
kumquat
orange
pepper, orange
persimmon
tangerine

PURPLE

cabbage, red
cherry
eggplant
fig
grape
onion
pepper, purple
plum
potato, red
radicchio

YELLOW

banana
grapefruit
lemon
peach
pepper, yellow
pineapple
squash, summer

WHITE

cauliflower
mushroom
onion
squash, scallop

GREEN

apple
artichoke
avocado
banana
broccoli
brussels sprout
celery
fennel
fig
gooseberry
grape
kale
lime
pepper, green
plum
squash

viburnum, or hydrangeas to fill in the empty spaces. I also like to take any fading flowers that still have some color and hang them upside down until they're dry, to use in potpourri.

No discussion about arranging flowers would be complete without including some of the other options. Fruits and vegetables, either by themselves or combined with flowers, offer almost endless possibilities. The results can often be spectacular—and very unexpected! When I think of a Victorian dinner table, I always envision towering silver épergnes with luscious fruits, bonbons, and flowers spilling from one tier to the next. Or ornate platters of fruits, with flowers tucked among them. It's easy to understand why this custom is becoming popular again. Just consider all the beautiful textures, shapes, and especially the colors of fruits and vegetables at any country market. The deep purple of eggplants, the rich red of ripe strawberries, the crisp yellow of big lemons. To help you introduce them into your flower arrangements, I've included a list of fruits and vegetables, organized by color.

☙ **ABOVE LEFT: A garden celebration of green and white! Here, savoy cabbage leaves line a basket filled with cauliflower, artichokes, and bridal wreath.**

☙ **OPPOSITE: It's an old French country custom to put a bowl of fragrant lemons or limes in a guest room to purify the air. My touch—a liner of hosta and spearmint-scented costmary leaves.**

A simple bowl of polished fruits and nuts, or a colorful basket of baby carrots, new asparagus, tiny radishes, and yellow cherry tomatoes can be surprisingly stylish. Some fruits and vegetables, such as squash, tomato, and eggplant, provide their own flowers. And hollowed-out pumpkins, melons, oranges, and even limes can be fanciful containers—not only for flowers but for ice cream, sorbet, berries, dips, and many other foods.

When using fruits and vegetables, you should just use common sense. Make sure the produce you choose is blemish-free and as fresh as possible. (If it's not, it won't be appealing to the eye *or* the nose!) Wash and thoroughly dry or polish it before you arrange.

Consider the season when selecting and think in terms of spring asparagus, summer berries—or autumn gourds lined up on a mantelpiece for Thanksgiving. The idea for this celery tree came from a clever display of vegetables by the National Farmers Union at the Chelsea Flower Show in London.

❧ **What you will need for a Celery Tree.**

CELERY TREE

A good example of how an ordinary vegetable can be transformed into an unexpected centerpiece for the table. (Try this idea with asparagus, too!)

You will need:

1 10-inch terra-cotta dish
1 bunch of parsley
2 feet of masking tape
5 bunches of celery
2 yards of twine
2 cups of fine stones
1 cup of water

1. Cut parsley stems to 3 inches in length.
2. Cut tape in half so it will be easier to manage. Tape parsley sprigs around the inside circumference of the dish.
3. With a sharp knife, trim the base of each celery bunch evenly so the stalks sit level and do not separate.
4. Using twine, tie the bunches together at the top, just under the leaves.
5. Have someone hold the celery upright in the center of the dish while you pour the stones all around to support it.
6. Add the cup of water to the dish, and freshen when necessary.

Another easy way to arrange vegetables is in baskets, like the following.

❧ **A finished Celery Tree centerpiece.**

PEPPER BASKET

A clever idea for using peppers, or other nicely shaped vegetables like squash, tomatoes, or eggplant, or even fruits like pears or pomegranates.

> *Basket*
> *An assortment of*
>   *colorful peppers*
> *Red lettuce leaves*
> *Block of brown floral foam*
> *Flower picks*

1. Choose a basket with a nice texture. Polish peppers with a dishcloth, and separate some lettuce leaves.
2. Wedge a block of brown floral foam securely in the basket and cover it with the lettuce.
3. Insert one end of the flower pick into a pepper and insert the other end into the foam, attaching the pepper to it. Build your arrangement by alternating the colors, filling the whole basket from left to right.
4. Insert some lettuce leaves between the peppers to fill any spaces.
5. Build up the center by adding as many peppers as you need to make an attractive composition, using picks to attach the peppers to each other.

When working with fruits and vegetables, carefully consider their texture, size, and shapes. Opt for variety. Buy small apples, medium oranges, and little berries and use them all together. Use fruits with interesting shapes, like bananas, pineapples, figs, grapes, and the endless varieties of squash. And don't forget to include things with interesting surfaces, such as cauliflower, artichokes, or gourds.

Experiment and learn to look at familiar standbys in new ways. Instead of using a whole melon, cut it in half, or peel a tangerine and add it to the composition of a centerpiece. For starters, you could follow the step-by-step instructions for making the Pepper Basket and the Celery Tree on these pages.

In the *Alice B. Toklas Cookbook,* the author remarks that, "The first gathering of the garden in May of salads, radishes, and herbs made me feel like a mother about her baby—how could anything so beautiful be mine?" And they are beautiful! Just walking by a fruit market always inspires me with wonderful new ideas.

⋛🐚 **A finished fresh Pepper Basket.**

FINISHING

TOUCHES

CHAPTER

When I was working on my first little book, *A Token of Friendship,* there were so many wonderful quotes I wanted to use but didn't have enough room for. I did, however, save one that I like to use on the gift cards I put with the fresh garden bouquets I give to friends: "As the Flowers in our Gardens, so are our Friends in our Lives."

Friends and flowers both are to be treasured. And when it comes to expressions of our affection for special friends or anyone we care about, I think that flowers are the nicest thing we can give. Indeed, there is nothing that I appreciate more. Whether it's a bouquet from a florist, or an armful of blossoms gathered from the garden, it doesn't matter. Each has its own charm.

In this chapter, I will discuss how you can make the flowers you give even more appealing by wrapping and presenting them in special ways. With the simple addition of fabric or paper, and some beautiful ribbon, a swathe of lace, or other touches, you can transform your gift into something more personal that tells the recipient how much you care.

The next time you come across a picture by the eighteenth-century painters Joshua Reynolds, Jean Honoré Fragonard, or François Boucher, notice the bows and ribbons—exceptional ribbons of glowing satin and silk and paper-thin taffeta—shown adorning the hair, the wrists, and of course, the flowers. You'll find that trimmings enhance flowers tremendously. Look for unusual kinds of rib-

bons, like wired ones, or embroidered ribbons with picot edging, or ribbons woven with flowers, plaids, or checks. I always prefer using good-quality ribbons, and have found pretty, often old ones at tag sales where they've been tucked into old sewing baskets. Remember that ribbons should complement, not overpower, the colors of the flowers.

You can also have fun with lace, raffia, and string of different textures and widths. Try using several bows layered on top of one another. And when cutting the ends, snip them at different lengths so their tendrils trail gracefully.

And don't forget the difference a little piece of fabric can make. Wrap a round vase in a square of fabric, tuck the ends into the rim, and secure them with floral tape. (This is also a clever way to disguise a humble jam jar.) Or place a simple glass bud vase in the center of an antique lace hankie, gather the corners around the neck of the vase, and tie them in place with frothy, wired ribbon. By presenting your flowers this way, the hankie becomes part of the gift!

And here's a marvelous idea for sprucing up a flower pot—swag it with a length of elegant fabric like moiré, silk faille, or paper taffeta. Simply follow the easy instructions on page 86:

〜 OVERLEAF: Old and new ribbons to embellish and enhance gifts of flowers.

〜 OPPOSITE: A simple vase of flowers transformed by a ribbon-tied hankie.

ELEGANT FLOWER POTS

Terra-cotta pot
Fabric
Masking tape
Straight pins
Florist wire (medium #24)

1. Measure the circumference of the top of the pot. Cut the fabric so it's twice as long as your measurement, and 12 inches wide. (I used a pot 21 inches around, so I needed fabric that was 42 inches long.)
2. Lay the fabric flat on a table, wrong side up. Fold both sides into the center, and tape closed. (This side goes against the pot, so the tape won't be seen.)
3. Mark with pins 2 inches in from each end of the fabric. Determine the length you want each scallop to be, confining

☙ ABOVE LEFT: Elegant swags surround a terra-cotta pot filled with carnations. And, above, all the makings you will need to create pretty swags for your own pots.

your measurements between these two end-pins. Mark the length of each scallop so that the fabric between the two end-pins is divided in equal parts. (Each pin marks a gathering point of the swag.)

4. Cut the florist wire into 6-inch pieces so that you have one piece for each gathering point. Starting at one end, remove the marking pin, and tie a piece of wire tightly around the fabric at that point, twisting it several times. These twisted ends will be hooked over the rim of the top of the pot.

5. Hook the first wire over the rim, then continue hooking each wire until the last wire ends up meeting the first, and the two end pieces of the swag overlap.

6. Secure the wire hooks to the inside of the pot with masking tape. For a clean finish, tuck the two loose fabric ends inside the pot, and anchor them firmly in place with masking tape.

ABOVE RIGHT: Flowers beautifully wrapped in cellophane and ribbon. ABOVE: A friendship posy that includes ranunculus, which means ''delicate pleasures.''

Of course, we all think of giving flowers on holidays and special occasions like Valentine's Day, Mother's Day, birthdays, and so on. But I especially like to give them when they are least expected. In fact, I've found that the little bouquets I give on "nonoccasions" are often the most appreciated because they *are* unexpected. For example, what better way to cheer a faraway or sick friend than with a "Language of Flowers" bouquet with blossoms that were carefully chosen to convey specific sentiments?

Flowers are also a welcome surprise when they are used as a decoration for other gifts. Tie some colorful flower sprigs onto a gift-wrapped present, or a book, or a bottle of champagne. Entwine leaves and ribbons around the handle of a thank-you basket that you've filled with sachets, cookies, or homemade jams. By the simple addition of flowers, as well as a simple addition *to* them, you make your gift more festive—and more memorable.

Still another way of adding a finishing touch to your bouquet is by wrapping it in a cone of tissue paper in various tints that echo the color of the flowers, then tying it up with ribbon in coordinating tints. For a less formal look—for a bunch of country flowers, for example—you can use recycled newspaper or craft paper and string for wrapping. And bouquets always look sophisticated when wrapped in cellophane tied with lots and lots of satin or silk ribbon.

It's also nice to use cellophane in a very special way. If you're invited to a dinner party and have your heart set on bringing flowers, you can wrap them in a cellophane vase that stands by itself. The advantage is that your host doesn't have to spend time away from his or her guests to hunt for a vase or arrange the flowers. The bouquet, sheathed in stiff cellophane, stands upright on its own. When I was in England the last time, I ordered one of these bouquets from Edward Goodyear, the official florist to the Queen. It was a beautiful addition to a small luncheon. Instructions on how you can make one are on the facing page:

❧ **At left, a tied bouquet of freesias, dianthus, sweet peas, roses, and ivy from Edward Goodyear, a London florist. At right, the same bouquet is wrapped, without being rearranged, in a cellophane vase that can be immediately set on a table.**

🌿 It's easy to construct a standing cellophane vase. The only supplies you need are flowers, garden twine, stiff florist cellophane, paper clips, and some ribbon.

STANDING CELLOPHANE VASE

Flowers
Garden twine
Stiff cellophane
Paper clips
Ribbon

1. Loosely hold the flowers in the center with one hand, and arrange them with the other, as if in a vase. When you achieve the desired effect, tie the flowers together with twine (as shown on the *opposite page, far left*).

2. Cut two 24-inch pieces from a roll of cellophane. Neatly fold each piece width-wise into 1-inch accordion pleats. Then secure each one in the center with a paper clip.

3. Place the bouquet flat on a table, with the stems toward you. Lay one piece of the pleated cellophane against each side of the bouquet (as shown *above*). Then tie the bouquet and cellophane together at the center, removing the paper clips.

4. Trim the flower stems and cellophane at bottom to an even length. Press the bouquet down slightly to stand it on a table. The stiff cellophane will hold the bouquet upright (as shown, *near left*).

5. After the dinner or luncheon, the bouquet should not be rearranged. Instead, the cellophane should be removed, the stems re-cut, and the flowers placed in a water-filled vase.

POTTED

PLANTS

A flowering plant brings a breath of spring into the home in winter. Clay pots on a kitchen windowsill provide us with cooking herbs, whatever the season. And some house plants supply foliage for cut flower arrangements all year long.

When choosing plants, however, we tend to limit our selection to the expected—philodendrons, palms, ficus, asparagus ferns, begonias, and the like. But there are many other choices available that we could and should consider.

Take orchids, for example. Most people do not know that orchids are *the* largest family of flowering plants. There are many beautiful varieties that are easy to grow, and that will thrive and bloom profusely indoors with minimal care.

If there's a cool corner you'd like to fill, consider a bay laurel tree. It's hardy indoors, and can survive on two hours of sunlight a day. (A bonus is that you can use the fresh bay leaves in cooking.)

Indoor fruit trees, grown primarily for their ornamental foliage, produce edible fruit with proper care. Kumquat, dwarf lemon, lime, orange, tangerine, and even figs top the list—some even produce fragrant flowers.

Try growing a precious Japanese bonsai or an elegant topiary of ivy, lavender, or rosemary, which can be trained into sculptured shapes of all sizes.

At Christmas, there are many miniature evergreens, including dwarf spruces and hollies, that can be placed around the house. In spring, they can be planted outdoors to be enjoyed for years to come.

Other flowering house plant possibilities include camellia, clivia, fuchsia, fragrant scented geraniums, passionflower, and jasmine. Also, don't forget garden flowers. Primroses, pansies, and forget-me-nots are just some of the spring flowers that bloom sweetly indoors and can be planted outdoors later.

Potted plants are living things that are sensitive to their environment. They must be properly cared for and cherished to stay healthy and survive. We all know someone who has that fortunate ability to make plants thrive. Perhaps the explanation lies in this lovely thought from *The Education of a Gardener* by landscape designer and garden writer Russell Page:

To have "green fingers" or a "green thumb" is an old expression which describes the art of communicating the subtle energies of love to prosper a living plant. . . . If you wish to make anything grow you must understand it, and understand it in a very real sense. "Green fingers" are a fact, and a mystery only to the unpracticed. But green fingers are the extensions of a verdant heart.

🌿 **OVERLEAF: Lily-of-the-valley pips that were forced indoors at the Cloisters, a unique Manhattan museum featuring medieval art and inspiring gardens.**

🌿 **OPPOSITE: Crowd all your primrose pots into one country basket lined with moss until you're ready to transplant them in your garden in late spring.**

❧ Indoor gardens created by, left, ivy, ferns, and angel-wing begonia, in a cast-iron urn; and, right, topiaries of white lavender and English ivy trained on wire forms. OPPOSITE: Growing elegant orchids like these is easier than you'd expect.

Before purchasing a plant, always discuss its care, and read the directions that may come with it. Be sure you're fully informed about the following:

Sunlight—Plants need proper sunlight so consider the exposure of the room in which you put them. Grow-lights can be used to augment natural light.

Air temperature—Most plants like temperatures from 55° to 60° F. Though most homes are warmer and drier than this, a humidifier helps. Room temperature should be maintained as evenly as possible and the plant kept out of drafts.

Watering—Too much watering is as bad as too little. Know what's required and only water as needed.

Misting—This is effective for most plants, as is wiping dirt and atmospheric pollution from leaves with a damp sponge (plants need fresh air). In summer, put your plants outside in the rain.

Potting soil—Always use bacteria-free soil. Watch for disease and insects, and deal with them immediately.

If you're having problems with your plant, call the place where you bought it or your local garden center for advice.

You can put your plants in anything from rustic flower pots to elegant cache-pots. Or, if you prefer to keep the plant in its original pot, pop it into a thatchy basket and cover the soil with moss. I like terra-cotta flower pots, especially the traditional English ones with the narrow rims. I sometimes leave my pots outdoors in winter or bury them in a corner of the garden in spring. Months later, when retrieved, they're mottled and moldy looking—just the effect I wanted.

You can lift your spirits in the bleak winter months after Christmas by filling your house with blooming amaryllis, crocuses, hyacinths, paper white narcissus, freesias, and tulips. Forcing bulbs—coaxing flowers to bloom out of their normal season—is easy to do.

The first thing to remember is that these bulbs require cold treatment before they will bloom indoors. Flats or pots planted outside or stored in a cool basement need 8 to 12 weeks at 40°–50° F., depending upon the bulb, in order to bloom. If, like me, you don't want to be bothered, you can order pre-cooled bulbs ready to bloom, through many mail-order catalogues and nurseries.

There are three methods of forcing bulbs: in pebbles, in soil, or in water. The water method is simplest. Pre-cooled bulbs of hyacinths, crocuses, and narcissus should be placed in forcing vases filled to the neck—not the brim—with water. Position the bulb with tip up and the base touching the water. The roots will grow decoratively, curling into the base of the vase, and in one to two months, depending upon the bulb, you'll have fragrant flowers. Check with your local nursery, because in fall you may be able to plant some of the bulbs outside.

Forcing branches from flowering trees and bushes is another way of hastening the onset of spring. Whatever you choose—cherry, crabapple, dogwood, forsythia, magnolia, peach, pear, plum, pussywillow, or quince—the closer you

cut them to their normal spring-flowering time, the sooner the flowers will open. But if you're impatient, like me, cut them anytime from January on, after several months of cold weather.

• Choose branches with buds about to swell, and cut them cleanly with sharp pruning shears. Keep the shape in mind, because what you're really doing is pruning the bush.

• Bring the branches indoors at once. Re-cut the ends on a slant, and hammer each to increase the flow of water to the buds.

• Place the branches in a vase of warm water, topped off regularly, and spray the branches with warm water to simulate spring rain.

• Don't place the vase in drafts or direct sunlight.

• The branches will take from several weeks to two months to flower. To speed the process, re-cut stem ends and change water more frequently.

🌿 **OPPOSITE: Crates of fragrant hyacinths ready to be repotted remind me of the words written by Thomas Jefferson in 1766 in his famous *Garden Book*. "March 30. Purple hyacinth begins to bloom." This was the very first line of the planting and flowering records he kept for fifty-eight years.**
🌿 **ABOVE RIGHT: Hyacinths bloom in hand-blown, cobalt Victorian forcing vases.**

SILK AND POR

CELAIN **F**LOWERS

CHAPTER

Artificial flowers are often subject to controversy. People either love them or dislike them intensely. Part of the problem, I think, is that those who are averse to artificial flowers make the mistake of comparing them to live flowers and then finding them wanting.

For some people, artificial flowers may evoke the familiar images seen in Victorian engravings of the wool and beadwork blooms often displayed under large glass domes. Or, perhaps the dusty wax or porcelain arrangement they once encountered in a corner of an antiques shop. Or today's mass-market, lifeless-looking plastic flowers, whose artificiality is all too apparent.

But nothing could be further from what this chapter will discuss—that is, artificial flowers of quality, beauty, and real craftsmanship. Such flowers can have a charm all their own. And they can be especially useful at those times of the year when your choice of affordable fresh flowers may be limited.

Whether the flowers are made of silk, beads, straw, paper, or porcelain, always buy the best ones you can find. Just as with fresh flowers, you will get what you pay for. Keep in mind that artificial flowers are a decorative accessory you'll be living with for a long time, so if you choose them with taste and discretion, you'll enjoy them for many years.

How long do they last? That depends. Artificial flowers need to be maintained. In *The Scented Room,* I mentioned this in reference to dried flowers,

which should be dusted and kept away from direct sunlight to prevent their fading. And the same goes for artificial flowers. When the blooms start to look faded or unattractively old, they should be replaced immediately.

Artificial flowers have been enjoyed for centuries. In England, the Georgians surrounded themselves with flowers of every material, and the concept of botanically correct painted silk flowers stems from this period. In 1772, Mary Granville Delany began creating her paper flower "mosaicks." These were exquisite collages made from hundreds of tints of tissue paper that she cut into shapes of petals, leaves, and stems, and glued to a black background. During her lifetime, she made almost a thousand of these little floral masterpieces. In 1789, the year after Mrs. Delany died, the classicist Erasmus Darwin wrote:

So now DELANY forms her mimic bowers,
Her paper foliage, and her silken flowers;
Her virgin train the tender scissors ply,
Vein the green leaf, the purple petal dye.

&❧ OVERLEAF: Glorious, lush earthenware pansies, roses, morning glories, pomegranates, and figs—all by Clare Potter and arranged in a silver basket.
&❧ OPPOSITE: More examples of the artist's work surrounded by the models for them—hundreds of botanical photographs pinned to her studio walls.

Today Mrs. Delany's creations can be seen in the British Museum, and many years later are a joy to behold.

Beaded flowers date back to fifteenth-century Italy and the glassworks on the island of Murano in Venice. And in mid-eighteenth-century France, Madame de Pompadour zealously backed the porcelain factory, Vincennes, which later became Sèvres. In the middle of winter, she filled her garden at Bellevue with porcelain flowers and invited King Louis XV to visit. It was only when he stopped to pick one that he realized the flowers were porcelain and not real. (I love to imagine what they must have looked like!)

Contemporary artisan Clare Potter had no idea she was reaching back to a rich tradition when she started making ceramic flowers and fruits. This was after she began taking pottery classes in England, where she lived for a time with her family because of her husband's business. Now, in her Long Island studio, she's busy crafting beautiful botanical objects for private clients all over the world. Although her ceramic masterpieces include fruits and vegetables, flowers are what she loves the most. In her studio, there are snapshots of thousands of flowers pinned in rows to the walls because as she says, you must "know the flowers." And when you look at the finished results of her work—whether it's a single morning glory or a large basket filled with a mass of earthenware blossoms—you can believe that flowers are her greatest love.

Whenever I'm in Paris, I always make a stop at Maison Trousselier on the Boulevard Haussmann. The shop has been there for decades, and entering it is like stepping back into another time. It is a cornucopia of luscious varieties of every flower imaginable, and the colors just take your breath away. Like Louis XV, you must peer very closely to realize that they are, in fact, silk. If you're lucky enough to catch a glimpse of the back room, you will see walls lined with wooden boxes like card catalogues in a library, only

these boxes are filled with petals and leaves. Each silken leaf and petal is shaped and hand-painted, and a small bouquet is an investment that will give you pleasure for many years to come.

In *The Secret Garden,* by Frances Hodgson Burnett, Mary says that she feels she has found a world all her own. That's exactly the way I feel when I visit Maxine Hoff's London studio, which is filled to overflowing with silk flowers. Maxine formerly worked as display manager for Colefax and Fowler, the renowned English interior decorating firm, and in the film industry, but a lifelong interest in gardening led her to create a business that owes its success to the extraordinary

ABOVE: An antique painting inspires a craftsman tinting silk petals at Maison Trousselier in Paris, where the flowers, opposite, were created. At left are bunches of perfect roses waiting to be painted. At right are pink and deep purple silk anemones, looking as if freshly picked from the garden.

way she paints silk flowers. She's inspired by eighteenth-century Dutch still lifes, and the charming "florist's flowers" (including ranunculus, tulips, carnations, and auriculas) that the Huguenots brought to England when they were expelled from France.

With meticulous applications of watercolor, Maxine achieves the subtle shadings and beautiful detail work for which her flowers are internationally famous. And the natural way she arranges the flowers afterward is further evidence of her wonderful eye and taste.

One of her secrets is to dip the silk blossoms into murky tea once or twice before painting them. Tea softens the color to give them an aged, natural look. After the flowers are dry and painted, she works the petals and stems into natural shapes and positions using real flowers and antique flower engravings as a guide.

If the idea intrigues you, here's how you can paint your own fabric flowers:

PAINTED FABRIC FLOWERS

Real flowers or
illustrated flower books
Fabric flowers
Teabags
Watercolors
Watercolor brushes

1. Buy white or off-white fabric flowers. (Silk is best, but you can also use cotton or polyester.)
2. Boil water in a saucepan, and use 2 teabags to make tea as dark as possible. Dip only the flower head into the hot tea and soak for several minutes.
3. Hang each flower upside down until dry. If it's not dark enough, dip it again in hot tea. The flowers must be thoroughly dry before you paint them.
4. Dilute the watercolors you want to use to the palest tints possible (you can always darken them later, if needed), and paint the entire flower with its base color. Let dry thoroughly.
5. Using a darker shade of the base color, repaint the flower with uneven strokes so it looks natural. Let dry thoroughly.
6. Use a drier, finely pointed brush to paint in sharp details with undiluted, almost opaque color. Flowers must be thoroughly dry before you arrange them.

&❧ OPPOSITE LEFT: All that you'll need to paint fabric flowers of your own, including assorted botanical illustrations, white silk flowers, tea, paintbox, and brushes.
&❧ OPPOSITE RIGHT: Every nook and cranny of Maxine Hoff's studio in London is filled with her beautiful hand-painted silk flowers. They, and the arrangements she makes from them (like the bouquet, above, displayed in a Victorian earthenware vase), are inspired by the lush art of eighteenth-century Dutch flower painters.

FINDING THE

BEST FLOWERS

CHAPTER

As I've often mentioned throughout this book, the quality and condition of the flowers you use will make a big difference in the way your arrangement looks. Even if you have your own cutting garden, there may be times when you will want to augment what you grow with bought flowers. This chapter will help you to find the best flowers available.

The range of places where you can purchase flowers and plants is continually expanding, so you'll have lots of choices. The possibilities cover everything from your neighborhood florist, for placing an order for a large party, to your local greengrocer, where you can pick up a last-minute bouquet for an intimate dinner. Even better (or perhaps not, if you have trouble making decisions), it's possible these days to buy almost any type of flower out of season.

Take advantage of all these wonderful opportunities, and let the flowers inspire you. Take Helen Keller's comment to heart: "Smell the perfume of the flowers. . . . Make the most of every sense. Glory in all the facets and pleasures and beauty which the world reveals to you."

 Florists

The term was first used in the seventeenth century when these botanical specialists cultivated the "florist flowers." Carnations, tulips, anemones, and ranunculus were the first such flowers to be listed, then later, auriculas, hyacinths, polyanthus, pinks, pansies, and dahlias were added. Modern florists, as we know them, emerged in the late nineteenth century, first selling potted plants and then cut flowers.

You might wonder why anyone would go to a florist when flowers are now readily available in so many different locations (including convenient street corners). One important reason is taste and quality. Florists are much more reliable because, as a rule, they stock the healthiest and best-quality flowers obtainable, and they condition them properly so that they will last longer after you get them home. It's true that you may find bargains elsewhere, but a too reasonable price could indicate that the flowers are not fresh, and thus won't last as long as ones purchased from a good florist.

꿀 OVERLEAF: In London, a sun-splashed view of the Museum of Garden History.
꿀 OPPOSITE, TOP LEFT: Bright poppies at Pure Mädderlake. TOP RIGHT: White and yellow flowers fill wire planters at Pulbrook & Gould. CENTER LEFT: Flower pots in the shade at Jane Packer's charming shop. CENTER RIGHT: At Salou, a florist cooler of brilliant mixed blossoms. BOTTOM LEFT: A forest of flowering branches at Zezé. BOTTOM CENTER: Inside Caroline Dickenson's shop—roses and carnations range from pink to red. BOTTOM RIGHT: A flower-filled wheelbarrow at Spring St. Garden.

🌜 The next eight photographs are examples of flowers arranged at their best by famous florists. ABOVE: This pretty country basket filled with viburnum, Mariella roses, white lilacs, ranunculus, and Icelandic poppies, was fashioned by designer Renny Reynolds, whose shop is located on New York City's exclusive Upper East Side. There, you'll find beautiful things, cut flowers and potted plants, including the lush, sophisticated, subtly colored arrangements that are Renny's trademark.

Convenience is another reason for patronizing a florist—especially if you use the same one regularly. If you do, he will be more inclined to order special flowers or foliage for you on request. And if you've chosen one with taste similar to yours, you'll find that you can always trust him to come up with something special if you are not able to visit the shop. I am also very particular when I send flowers to someone. With a good florist you can feel confident that a gift of flowers ordered over the phone will be selected and put together with taste.

Years ago, I found myself sitting in a friend's hospital room wondering who had sent a particularly awful arrangement. Imagine how I felt when I found out it was me! This experience taught me a lesson. Now, whenever I'm sending flowers outside my florist's delivery zone,

I always ask him if he can recommend someone in that area. This way, I know my taste level will be maintained. On the other hand, if no suggestions are forthcoming, I call several florists myself. And even then, I always try to keep it simple and am very specific as to the kinds of flowers, their colors, and the type of vase or basket I prefer.

New York City is one of those places that's filled with wonderful florists and floral designers, each having his or her own point of view. I like to look in their windows, walk around their shops, and ask questions. I suggest you do the same in your area. You're sure to find one you like. Below are some that I like!

Renny Reynolds' flower shop is located in one of the most exclusive streets on the Upper East Side. When you enter, you feel as though you're in an Italian

New York City's fine florists include Pure Mädderlake, where you can expect to find something different, like the cheerful country bouquet, left, of white stock, phlox, tulips, ranunculus, viburnum, and poppies wrapped in craft paper and ready to go. RIGHT: From Zezé in New York City, here are flowers that are lavish and utterly dramatic. An elegant, ornately colored ceramic vase is filled to overflowing with brightly colored roses, parrot and pencil tulips, peonies, dahlias, and fritillaria.

palazzo filled with everything from topiaries to tulips. Renny is particularly noted for the beautifully subtle colors that he uses when putting flowers together in his very abundant arrangements.

Pure Mädderlake is housed in a high-ceilinged space in Soho where Tom Pritchard and Billy Jarecki stock gift ideas and accessories in addition to their fresh flower selections. Everywhere you look there is something to catch the eye. They specialize in arranging flowers that look as if they have just come from a garden.

Zezé's flower shop, near the East River, is like a tiny, verdant corner of a forest. Zezé is a charming Frenchman who likes to use lavish, romantic flowers. He sometimes arranges them in antique urns set between the bowers of branches that fill his shop and spill out onto the sidewalk, creating a botanical fantasy.

Pat Braun and Stephen Lilie are the talented proprietors of Salou, one flight down in a wonderful vintage building on the Upper West Side. Their arrangements have a very natural style, and often, they'll cut long-stemmed varieties of flowers very short, giving them a totally different look. When they finish arranging them in one of their little vases, the flowers resemble precious jewels.

Spring St. Garden in Soho is one of the coziest flower shops in New York. An old wheelbarrow filled with all sorts of plants greets you at the door and beckons you inside. The affable owner, Rita Bobry, has some of the most beautiful flowers in town. Her bouquets typically are filled with an abundance of blossoms and tied with lots of ribbons—charming, cheerful, and often, delightfully unexpected. (You can see one in Chapter 5.)

❧ Salou, on New York's Upper West Side, is known for very special-looking bouquets like this one of delicate flowers, including roses, astilbe, and ranunculus in a Majolica cup and saucer.

❧ Sophisticated and elegant are the words to describe the work of Lisa Krieger. Composed in this graceful vase are plume celosia, snapdragons, dahlias, sunflowers, and billowy roses.

Interior and garden designer Lisa Krieger was once the Associate Curator of Gracie Mansion. Her training, tempered by a romantic style, influences the way she works with flowers—whether it's a naive bunch of pansies or a sophisticated collection of roses. She brings to all the graceful hand that is also reflected in the tasteful interiors of both her home and studio in Connecticut.

J. Barry Ferguson, originally from New Zealand, works on Long Island, and his approach to flowers is eclectic. "One must learn to be beautiful and practical," he says, and anyone who has seen the beauty that he creates for the Winter Antiques Show in Manhattan every January will know what he means. Known for his large arrangements, he leaves his own special signature on everything he does.

In London, Caroline Dickenson's shop on Berkeley Square is very cool and modern. Her flower-arranging style, however, is almost the opposite. She's a cheerful woman who enjoys working with vibrant colors, a wide range of flowers, and fruits and vegetables in her creative and innovative designs.

During their thirty-plus years in business, Pulbrook & Gould, one of the most tasteful florists in London, has developed ties with small gardeners and flower growers throughout England who supply them with normally unobtainable botanicals. As a result, the inside of their shop looks like a sumptuous English country garden. Partner Sonja Waites says they like to arrange flowers to look as natural as possible, with each blossom as perfect as it can be.

The venerable florist Edward Goodyear is a London fixture sitting between two of my favorite places, Colefax and Fowler and Claridge's. Aside from their

👤 ABOVE: At her shop in London's Berkeley Square, Caroline Dickenson creates bouquets of abundance. This one includes snowberry, hawthorn, morning glory, rose, peony, delphinium, and eggplant. BELOW: From Pulbrook & Gould, one of London's most renowned florists, a bouquet in a distinctive combination of purple and orange—hosta, cornflower, Solomon seal, yarrow, sweet pea, and an arum lily.

fame as the official posy makers for Buckingham Palace, they're also known for the special way they wrap them. (Chapter 7 shows how you can do it yourself.)

Other London favorites include Robert Day's shop that features an assortment of offerings including dried flowers, sometimes coordinated with sea shells, lichen, moss, and wonderful found objects, and Jane Packer's shop, which is filled with clever arranging ideas that she shares in classes at her flower school (you can sign up to learn the basics plus). And if you happen to be in Paris, be sure to stop in at Moulie Savart and other very special florists. (For addresses and phone numbers of the above mentioned and other florists, see the Source Directory.)

🦋 In J. Barry Ferguson's studio—a still life of clustered vases with flowers.

Wholesale Flower Markets

Many cities have wholesale flower markets or districts where, at the crack of dawn, you'll see caterers and restaurant owners, fashion stylists, and, of course, retail florists shopping for the best and freshest selections to use that day. Some of the largest include: the flower district in New York City on the West Side between 27th and 29th Streets (New York City is the port of entry for almost all European flowers, and many of these are sold in the flower district); the Los Angeles Flower Market on Maple Avenue in Los Angeles; the Covent Garden Flower Market, moved from its charming glass-covered premises to modern facilities in Southwest London, England; and its counterpart, Rungis, in Paris, France.

Though technically these markets are wholesale, some welcome retail buyers. When you're in a new city, check the yellow pages to see if there is a flower district nearby. The variety of flowers, as well as their freshness, is a good reason to visit. Of course, you can't just walk in and expect to buy a few daffodils. But when you do need a large quantity of flowers—as decoration for Christmas or a big party, for example—you can save money by buying directly at the source.

Your best bet is to plan ahead, know what you want, and buy in bunches. When you shop in a wholesale market, you may be asked for your resale number; if you don't have one, you will be charged tax. And in most cases, unless you are known, you'll have to pay cash. (Be sure to set your alarm very early; most of these markets open to the trade around dawn and are closed by noon.)

If you love flowers, then you must visit Holland. In Amsterdam, for example, every corner and windowbox, even houseboats on the canals, are overflowing with flowers, and in spring when all the tulips are in bloom, it's an unbelievable sight to behold!

While in Holland, be sure to save time for a visit to Aalsmeer, where the largest flower auctions in the world have been held since 1912. Every day, members of the Cooperative (there are almost 5,000 growers) deliver the flowers and plants they have gathered from their farms and nurseries in the early morning. The assorted flowers are then examined, documented, and brought into one of the six auction rooms available.

The Dutch have worked out a unique system in which the roster of international buyers, including florists, street vendors, and anyone whose business is selling flowers, can operate a switch on his or her seat in order to bid. The bid is then registered on a huge white-faced clock—whose figures represent sums of money—in front of the auction room. And while retail customers cannot buy flowers here, just viewing the auction is a fascinating experience. It also gives one an inside peek at the workings of the international flower industry.

🌿 ABOVE LEFT: At the wholesale flower market in New York City, fresh plants are set out early in the morning. Also worth visiting is the New Covent Garden flower market in London, where you'll find busy vendors and such delights as boxes of sweet William, right, and abundant bunches of tightly wrapped peonies, below.

 ## Outdoor Markets

In the United States, the trend of farmer's markets is growing in villages and cities everywhere. I love shopping for flowers in these markets. In New York City's Union Square, the farmer's market is open several days a week, which is a real treat. In spring, graceful branches of quince, forsythia, and magnolia are offered next to stalls filled with every kind of flowering bulb in bloom. In between the gorgeous flowers are stands selling fresh cheese, eggs, jams and jellies, and home-baked goods, all locally produced.

The open-air flower market on the Singel in Amsterdam is worth a visit. So is the Pont Neuf Flower Market in Place Louis Lepine and Quai de la Corse in Paris, where the sight of rows and rows of flowers against the backdrop of the river Seine and Notre Dame is something very special indeed.

One of the nicest things about traveling is being able to buy flowers from a corner kiosk, something I often do to make my hotel room feel more like home. In London, I especially love the delightful barrows, situated in familiar locations throughout the city, that usually offer wonderful varieties of flowers.

As I travel around our own country, I'm pleased to see more and more flowers and plants available at greengrocers and even in some supermarkets. But do be a smart shopper. The convenience of

🦋 RIGHT: There is something very special about the lively Pont Neuf Market on the Ile de la Cité. It is the oldest flower market in Paris, dating from 1808, and is always stocked with breathtaking flowers exploding in a riot of color. This is where I enjoy going to pick up delicate nosegays for my hotel room.

🦋 LEFT: The proprietor of one of the permanent stalls located in the Pont Neuf Market checks the weather in front of the bright green painted facade, the background for fragrant flowers that herald spring. In addition to flowers, you can also purchase potted plants, bulbs, and seeds for your home and garden.

buying in these places must be balanced with special attention to the condition and freshness of the flowers.

Nurseries and Garden Centers

I remember a time when I couldn't buy certain herbs anywhere near my home. Today, thank goodness, this has all changed, and there are many nurseries and garden centers where you can obtain interesting house plants and cut flowers, in addition to what you want to plant in your garden. Develop a rapport with the people at your local garden center. You'll find them a dependable source of information about plants and flowers.

Also see if there are any flower farms in your area. We have an anemone farm near us, and though they cater to the wholesale trade, a retail customer can still buy beautiful bunches of fresh flowers from them. Roadside flower stands are also worth a stop in summer.

When visiting gardens open to the public, I always check to see if they have a nursery or gift shop that sells seeds or plants. Some, like Winterthur in Delaware and Sissinghurst in Kent, England, carry a selection of seedlings from their gardens. Others, like Syon House, outside London, have large National Trust nurseries with everything for the flower gardener. But any visit to a garden offers inspiration and a laundry list of ideas you'll want to try.

🌿 **Scenes at the Chelsea Flower Show.**
TOP LEFT: A gaily striped awning marks the entrance to this annual show that covers a twenty-three-acre site on the grounds of the Royal Hospital. **TOP RIGHT:** A tiny narcissus sported in an exhibitor's buttonhole. **ABOVE LEFT:** The signs here are as tasteful and pretty as the flowers themselves. **ABOVE CENTER:** Cascades of ivy in more varieties than you'd think existed! **ABOVE RIGHT:** Fresh herbs surrounding a wagon, one of the unique exhibits that come from specialty farms all over England.

(Note: You can only bring plants back to the United States from abroad if you have a special permit, obtained before leaving home, from the U.S. Department of Agriculture in Hyattsville, Maryland.)

Flower Shows

Visiting a flower show can be an unforgettable experience. In the United States, there are excellent flower shows that I try to visit every year, including those in Seattle, Philadelphia, New York, and Boston. I always come away with lots of ideas, as well as seeds, seedlings, and, sometimes, cut flowers I use at home.

When I travel abroad, I try not to miss the Great Spring Flower Show of the Royal Horticultural Society, known as the Chelsea Flower Show since 1913, when it moved to that area of London. It's an extraordinary event, and tickets are always at a premium. However, if you join the Royal Horticultural Society (see the Source Directory in the back of the book), you may buy your tickets in advance with a minimum of fuss.

The show, usually the third week in May, is held in the Great Marquee, a huge tent covering almost four acres. The best, most spectacular flowers (including gorgeous roses), vegetables, fruits, herbs,

TOP LEFT: The Chelsea Flower Show excels in displays of old-fashioned roses. This vividly tinted example is called Comte de Chambord, which is a Portland rose first discovered in 1860. TOP RIGHT: A display of the Delphinium Society, one of the many flower organizations exhibiting their specialties at the show. ABOVE LEFT: A uniform display of rows of lupines. ABOVE RIGHT: A seemingly endless vista of cut flowers and potted plants, seen from inside the Great Marquee, a huge tent that takes up almost four acres of space.

🐚 ABOVE LEFT: Flower farms are a good source for cut flowers. Shown here, the greenhouse of a ranunculus farm near my home. ABOVE RIGHT: When groundsmen tidy the lawns of the Bagatelle gardens in Paris, their wheelbarrows soon overflow with rose petals (a sight that tempts me to gather them up for making potpourri!).

THE GARDEN IS
RATHER CROWDED.

The Shop & Tea Room
are open. Please visit
them first & enter
the Garden later.

🐚 The sign, above left, includes everything I love—gardens, shopping, and eating! It's at Sissinghurst, England, my favorite National Trust Garden. ABOVE RIGHT: Royal gardener, John Tradescant the Elder, with a basket of plants over his arm. The statue and the sampler, opposite, are at London's Museum of Garden History.

and greens are usually shown here, along with prize-winning flower arrangements. Surrounding the tent are hundreds of stalls exhibiting garden statuary and furniture, tools, seeds, botanical prints, antique and new books, garden equipment, greenhouses, and much more. There's also a series of small gardens crowded with plants that appeal and inspire. Wear comfortable shoes!

Another captivating place is London's Museum of Garden History set in St. Mary-at-Lambeth Church on the Thames. John Tradescant, who died in 1638, and his son John, are buried in its churchyard. Both were gardeners to English royalty, including Charles I. From their travels in America and Europe, they brought back many plants, trees, and shrubs that we take for granted today. Their collection of specimen plants, left to Elias Ashmole, forms the basis of Oxford's Ashmolean Collection.

By the 1970s, the church had become so run down it was to be demolished, until Rosemary Nicholson and her husband managed to set up the Tradescant Trust, which, with the backing of the British Royal Family, raised enough money to restore the church and garden.

It's a wonderful place to spend the morning or afternoon. After visiting the museum, stop in the little gift shop and then relax with a cup of tea. Later, take a leisurely stroll in the beautifully recreated seventeenth-century garden surrounded by ancient brick walls and filled with plants and flowers.

Isn't it reassuring, in a complex, often confusing world, to know that the simple, beautiful things in nature, like flowers, are here to soothe the spirit, just as they have always been. As Guy de Maupassant so tenderly said:

"Sometimes our thoughts turn back toward a corner in a forest, or the end of a bank, or an orchard powdered with flowers, seen but a single time on some gay day, yet remaining in our hearts and leaving a feeling that we have just rubbed elbows with happiness."

THERE IS PEACE WITHIN A GARDEN
A PEACE SO DEEP AND CALM
THAT WHEN THE HEART IS TROUBLED
IT'S LIKE A SOOTHING BALM

THERE'S LIFE WITHIN A GARDEN
A LIFE THAT STILL GOES ON
FILLING THE EMPTY PLACES
WHEN OLDER PLANTS HAVE GONE

THERE'S GLORY IN THE GARDEN
AT EVERY TIME OF YEAR
SPRING SUMMER AUTUMN WINTER
TO FILL THE HEART WITH CHEER

SO EVER TEND YOUR GARDEN
ITS BEAUTY TO INCREASE
FOR IN IT YOU'LL FIND SOLACE
AND IN IT YOU'LL FIND PEACE.

SOURCE

DIRECTORY

AUTHORS

"A book is like a garden carried in the pocket."
CHINESE PROVERB

I find it impossible to love flowers and not want to read about them. Twenty years ago at a library sale, I found a beautiful volume filled with color plates by Louise Beebe Wilder, and ever since I have been collecting old and contemporary flower and garden books. Below is a list of my favorite writers on these subjects. You might want to look for them when your local library has a sale, or at yard sales, church bazaars, and flea markets, or try the booksellers listed on the opposite page.

14TH TO 17TH CENTURY

Francis Bacon
Geoffrey Chaucer
John Evelyn
John Gerard
William Lawson
Bernard McMahon
Andrew Marvell
John Parkinson
Samuel Pepys
William Shakespeare
Thomas Tusser

18TH TO 19TH CENTURY

Liberty Hyde Bailey
Colette
William Cowper
Rev. George Crabbe
Alice Morse Earle
Shirley Hibberd
Dean Hole
Thomas Jefferson
Gertrude Jekyll

Mrs. Francis King
Charles Lamb
Jane W. Loudon
John C. Loudon
Alexander Pope
William Robinson
Eleanour Sinclair Rohde
Alfred, Lord Tennyson
Celia Thaxter
Henry David Thoreau
Horace Walpole
Edith Wharton
Louise Beebe Wilder

20TH CENTURY

Julia Berral
Wilfrid Blunt
E. A. Bowles
Jane Brown
Karel Capek
Beth Chatto
Alice M. Coates
Peter Coates
Fleur Cowles
Reginald Farrer
Helen Morgenthau Fox

Robin Lane Fox
Maude Grieve
Arthur Helleyer
David Hessayon
Penelope Hobhouse
Stephen Lacey
Allen Lacy
Elizabeth Lawrence
Ann Leighton
Mrs. C. F. Leyel
Betty Massingham
John Muir
Beverley Nichols
Russell Page
Allen Paterson
Eleanor Perenyi
Lanning Roper
Anne Scott-James
Sacheverell Sitwell
Constance Spry
Graham Stuart Thomas
Rosemary Verey
Vita Sackville-West
Katharine S. White
Frances Wolseley

BOOKSELLERS

Here are some favorite booksellers who feature books on flowers and gardening, both new and old.

UNITED STATES

American Botanist
1103 West Truitt Ave.
Chillicothe, IL 61523
(309) 274-5254

Anchor & Dolphin Books
30 Franklin St., Box 823
Newport, RI 02840
(401) 846-6890

Brooks Books
P.O. Box 21473
Concord, CA 94521
(415) 672-4566

Capability's Books
2379 Hwy. 46
Deer Park, WI 54007
1-800-247-8154

Barbara Farnsworth
P.O. Box 9
West Cornwall, CT 06796
(203) 672-6571

V. L. Green Booksellers
19 East 76th St.
New York, NY 10021
(212) 439-9194

Hurley Books
RR1, Box 160, Rte. 12
Westmoreland, NH 03467
(603) 399-4342

Landscape Books
Box 483
Exeter, NH 03833
(603) 964-9333

Lion's Head Books
Academy St.
Salisbury, CT 06068
(203) 435-9328

Timothy Mawson Books
New Preston, CT 06777
(203) 868-0732

Quest Rare Books
774 Santa Ynez
Stanford, CA 94305
(415) 324-3119

Savoy Books
Bailey Rd., Box 271
Lanesborough, MA 01237
(413) 499-9968

Second Life Books
Quarry Rd., Box 242
Lanesborough, MA 01237
(413) 447-8010

Stubbs Books & Prints
835 Madison Ave.
New York, NY 10021
(212) 772-3120

Wilkerson Books
31 Old Winter St.
Lincoln, MA 01773
(617) 259-1110

Elisabeth Woodburn
   Books
Box 398
Hopewell, NJ 08525
(609) 466-0522

CANADA

Pomona Book Exchange
Highway 52
Rockton, Ontario L0R 1X0
(519) 621-8897

ENGLAND

Hatchards
187 Piccadilly
London W1V
071-439-9921

Lloyds of Kew
9 Mortlake Terrace, Kew
Surrey TW9
940-2512

Potterton Books
The Old Rectory
Sessay
(0845) 401218

FRANCE

Librairie Maison Rustique
26, rue Jacob
Paris 75006
(1) 43-25-67-00

I especially want to add here a splendid garden magazine called Hortus, *which you will treasure like a book!*

HORTUS
The Neuadd, Rhayader
Powys LD6 5HH
Wales
44-597-810-227

Florists and Flower Shops

Below are some of the best-known, talented florists here and abroad.

UNITED STATES

J. Barry Ferguson Flowers
P.O. Box 176
Oyster Bay, NY 11771
(516) 922-0005

Lisa Krieger Gardens &
    Interiors
P.O. Box 221
Greens Farms, CT 06436
(203) 259-8571
    (by appointment)

Ronaldo Maia
27 East 67th St.
New York, NY 10021
(212) 288-1049

Marlo Flowers
428 A East 75th St.
New York, NY 10021
(212) 628-2246

Pure Mädderlake
478 Broadway
New York, NY 10013
(212) 941-7770

Renny
159 East 64th St.
New York, NY 10021
(212) 288-7000

Salou
105 West 72nd St.
New York, NY 10023
(212) 595-9604

Spring St. Garden
186½ Spring St.
New York, NY 10012
(212) 966-2015

Twigs
1305 Madison Ave.
New York, NY 10128
(212) 369-4000

VSF
204 West 10th St.
New York, NY 10014
(212) 206-7236

Dorothy Wako
15 West 26th St.
New York, NY 10010
(212) 686-5569
    (by appointment)

Zezé Flowers
398 East 52nd St.
New York, NY 10022
(212) 753-7767/7768

ENGLAND

Robert Day Flowers
89 Pimlico Road
London SW1
071-824-8655

Caroline Dickenson
    Flowers
55, Berkeley Square
London W1X
071-491-9494

Edward Goodyear
45 Brook St.
London W1
071-629-1508

Moyses Stevens
6 Bruton St.
London W1X
071-493-8171

Jane Packer Floral Design
56, James St.
London W1
071-935-2673

Pulbrook & Gould
127 Sloane St.
London SW1X
071-730-0030

Kenneth Turner
19 South Audley St.
London W1
071-499-2823

FRANCE

Arene
4 rue Mesnil
Paris 75016
47.27.32.19

Christian Tortu
6, Carrefour de l'Odeon
Paris 75006
43.26.02.56

La Chaume
10, rue Royale
Paris 75008
42.60.57.26/42.60.59.54

Moulie Savart
8, Place du Palais
    Bourbon
Paris 75007
45.51.78.43

FLOWER AND PLANT SOCIETIES

The organizations listed below can be fun and many offer a lecture series.

UNITED STATES

American Horticultural
  Society
7931 E. Boulevard Dr.
Alexandria, VA 22308
(703) 768-5700

American Rose Society
P.O. Box 30000
Shreveport, LA 71130
(318) 938-5402

Brooklyn Botanic Garden
1000 Washington Ave.
Brooklyn, NY 11225
(718) 622-4433

Garden Club of America
598 Madison Ave.
New York, NY 10022
(212) 753-8287

The Garden Conservancy
Box 219
Cold Spring, NY 10516
(914) 265-2029

Herb Society of America
9019 Kirland Chardon Rd.
Mentor, OH 44060
(216) 256-0514

Horticultural Society of
  New York
128 West 58th St.
New York, NY 10019
(212) 757-0915

New York Botanical Gardens
200 St. & Southern Blvd.
Bronx, NY 10458
(212) 220-8700

ENGLAND

The Cottage Garden Society
5 Nixon Close, Thornhill,
Dewsbury, W. Yorkshire
WF12 (0924) 468469

The Museum of Garden
  History
Lambeth Palace Road
London SE1
071-261-1891

Royal Horticulture
  Society
80 Vincent Square
London SW1P 2PE
071-834-4333

SILK AND PORCELAIN FLOWERS

If you love flowers as much as I do, you may want to speak with one of the people below, who specialize in ever-lasting bouquets.

UNITED STATES

Clare Potter
P.O. Box 624
Locust Valley, NY 11560
(516) 922-7957
Porcelain flowers

Anita Widder
Box 275
Old Westbury, NY 11568
(516) 229-2210
Silk flower arrangements

ENGLAND

Maxine Hoff
87 Black Lion Le.
London W6, England
081-748-7027
(*continued*)

and at:
A6370 Reith
Kitzbuehel
Mitterfeld 391 Austria
(05356) 59764
Silk flower arrangements

FRANCE

Maison Trousselier
73, blvd. Haussmann
75008 Paris, France
42.66.97.95
Silk flowers

Seed, Bulb, and Plant Catalogues

You can write to these mail-order companies for a catalogue. Most of them stock seeds, bulbs, and/or plants and many of them specialize.

UNITED STATES

Abundant Life Seed
    Foundation
P.O. Box 772
Port Townsend, WA
    98368
(206) 385-5660

Allen Sterling & Lothrop
    Seed Catalogue
191 U.S. Rte. 1
Falmouth, ME 04105
(207) 781-4742

Bluestone Perennials
7211 Middle Ridge Rd.
Madison, OH 44057
1-800-852-5243

Breck's
U.S. Reservation Center
6523 N. Galena Rd.
Peoria, IL 61632
(309) 691-4616

W. Atlee Burpee Co.
300 Park Ave.
Warminster, PA 18974
1-800-327-3049

Canyon Creek Nursery
3527 Dry Creek Rd.
Oroville, CA 95965
(916) 533-2166

Capriland's Herb Farm
Silver St.
Coventry, CT 06238
(203) 742-7244

Carroll Gardens
444 East Main St.
P.O. Box 310
Westminster, MD 21157
1-800-638-6334

Clifford's Perennial &
    Vine
Rte. 2, Box 320
East Troy, WI 53120
(414) 642-7156

Companion Plants
7247 North Coolville
    Ridge Rd.
Athens, OH 45701
(614) 592-4643

The Cook's Garden
P.O. Box 65
Londonderry, VT 05148
(802) 824-3400

Cooley's Gardens
11553 Silverton Rd. NE
Silverton, OR 97381
1-800-225-5391

The Country Garden
P.O. Box 3539
Oakland, CA 94609
(510) 658-8777

The Country Garden
Rte. 2, Box 455A
Crivitz, WI 45114

Dabney Herbs
Box 22061
Louisville, KY 40252
(502) 893-5198

Peter DeJagar Bulb Co.
188 Asbury St.
South Hamilton, MA
    01982
(508) 468-4707

Edible Landscaping
P.O. Box 77
Afton, VA 22920
(804) 361-9134

The Flowery Branch
P.O. Box 1330
Flowery Branch, GA
    30542
(404) 536-8380

The Fragrant Path
P.O. Box 328
Ft. Calhoun, NE 68023

Glasshouse Works
    Greenhouses
Church St., P.O. Box 97
Steward, OH 45778
(614) 662-2142

Grianan Gardens
P.O. Box 14492
San Francisco, CA 94114

Heard Gardens
5355 Merle Hay Rd.
Johnston, IA 50131
(515) 276-4533

Heirloom Garden Seeds
P.O. Box 138
Guerneville, CA 95446
(707) 869-0967

Heirloom Seeds
P.O. Box 245
W. Elizabeth, PA 15088
(412) 384-7816

Heirloom Vegetable
  Garden Project
157 Plant Science Bldg.
Cornell University
Ithaca, NY 14853
(607) 255-2241

The Herb Farm
Barnard Rd.
Granville, MA 01034
(413) 357-8882

Henry Field's Heritage
  Gardens
One Meadow Ridge Rd.
Shenandoah, IA 51601
(605) 665-1080

Indigo Knoll Perennial
16236 Compromise Ct.
Mount Airy, MA 21771
(301) 489-5131

J. L. Hudson, Seedsman
P.O. Box 1058
Redwood City, CA 94064

Thomas Jefferson Center
  for Historic Plants
P.O. Box 316
Charlottesville, VA 22902
(804) 979-5283

Johnny's Selected Seeds
Foss Hill Rd.
Albion, ME 04910
(207) 437-9294

J. W. Jung Seed Co.
335 South High St.
Randolph, WI 53957
(414) 326-4100

John Scheepers
R.D. 6, Philipsburg Rd.
Middletown, NY 10940
(914) 342-1135

Kartuz Greenhouses
1408 Sunset Dr.
Vista, CA 92083
(619) 941-3613

Klehm Nursery
Penny Rd.
South Barrington, IL
  60010
(708) 551-3720

Lauray of Salisbury
432 Undermountain Rd.
Salisbury, CT 06068
(203) 435-2263

Le Jardin du Gourmet
P.O. Box 75
St. Johnsbury Center, VT
  05863

Logee's Greenhouses
55 North St.
Danielson, CT 06239
(203) 774-8038

McClure & Zimmerman
108 W. Winnebago St.
Friesland, WI 53935
(414) 326-4220

Messelaar Bulb Co. Inc.
County Rd., P.O. Box 269
Ipswich, MA 01938
(508) 356-3737

Merry Gardens
Camden, ME 04843
(207) 236-9064

Netherland Bulb Co., Inc.
2 Cypress Peak Le.
Montvale, NJ 07645
(201) 391-0689

Nichols Garden Nursery
1190 North Pacific Hwy.
Albany, OR 97321
(503) 928-9280

Park Seed Company
Cokesbury Rd.
Greenwood, SC 29647
1-800-845-3369

Peace Seeds
2385 SE Thompson St.
Corvallis, OR 97333

Pinetree Garden Seeds
Rte. 100
New Gloucester, ME
  04260
(207) 926-3400

Plants of the Southwest
930 Baca St.
Santa Fe, NM 87501
(515) 983-1548

The Primrose Path
RD 2, Box 110
Scottdale, PA 15683
(412) 887-6756

Redwood City Seed Co.
P.O. Box 361
Redwood City, CA 94064
(415) 325-7333

Rhapis Gardens
Box 287
Gregory, TX 78359
(512) 643-2061

Russell Graham
4030 Eagle Crest Rd. NW
Salem, OR 97304
(503) 362-1135

The Sandy Mush Nursery
Rte. 2, Surrett Cove Rd.
Leicester, NC 28748
(704) 683-2014

Schreiner's Iris Gardens
3625 Quinaby Rd. NE
Salem, OR 97303
1-800-525-2367

Seeds Blüm
Idaho City Stage
Boise, ID 83706
(208) 342-0858

Seeds of Change
621 Old Santa Fe Trail
Santa Fe, NM 87501
(505) 983-8956

The Seed Source
Rte. 68, Box 301
Tuckasegee, NC 28783

Select Seeds
180 Stickney Hill Rd.
Union, CT 06076

Shepherd's Garden Seeds
30 Irene St.
Torrington, CT 06790
(203) 482-3638

R. H. Shumway Seedsman
P.O. Box 1
Graniteville, SC 29829
(803) 663-9771

Smith and Hawken
25 Corte Madera
Mill Valley, CA 94941
(415) 383-4415

Springhill
110 W. Elm St.
Tipp City, OH 45371
(513) 667-4079

Taylor's Herb Gardens
1535 Lone Oak Rd.
Vista, CA 92084
(619) 727-3485

Thompson & Morgan
P.O. Box 1308
Jackson, NJ 08527
(201) 363-2225

TyTy Plantation Bulb Co.
Box 159
TyTy, GA 31795
(912) 382-0404

K. Van Bourgondien
245 Farmingdale Rd.
Babylon, NY 11702
1-800-873-9444

Andre Viette Nursery
State Rte. 608, Box 16
Fishersville, VA 22939
(703) 943-2315

Village Arbors
1804 Saugahatchee Rd.
Auburn, AL 36830
(205) 826-3490

Wayside Gardens
Box 1
Hodges, SC 29695
1-800-845-1124

Well-Sweep Herb Farm
317 Mt. Bethel Rd.
Pt. Murray, NJ 07865
(908) 852-5390

White Flower Farm
Litchfield, CT 06759
1-800-888-7756

Willot Iris Garden
26231 Shaker Blvd.
Beachwood, OH 44122
(216) 831-8662

ROSE CATALOGUES

UNITED STATES

Antique Rose Emporium
Rte. 5, Box 143
Brenham, TX 77833
(409) 836-9051

Armstrong Roses
P.O. Box 4220
Huntington Sta., NY 11746
1-800-321-6640

Roses by Fred Edmunds
6235 S.W. Kahle Rd.
Wilsonville, OR 97070
(503) 638-4671

High Country Rosarium
1717 Downing
Denver, CO 80218
(303) 832-4026

Jackson & Perkins
1 Rose Le.
Medford, OR 97501
1-800-292-4769

Limberlost Roses
7304 Forbes Ave.
Van Nuys, CA 91406
(818) 901-7798

Lowe's Own-root Roses
6 Sheffield Rd.
Nashua, NH 03062
(603) 888-2214

Roses of Yesterday &
    Today
802 Brown's Valley Rd.
Watsonville, CA 95076
(408) 724-2755

SEEDS, BULBS, ROSES, AND PLANTS

CANADA

Aimers
81 Temperance St.
Aurora, Ontario L4G 2RI
(416) 833-5282

Gardenimport Inc.
P.O. Box 760
Thornhill, Ontario
   L3T 4A5
(416) 731-1950

Pickering Nurseries Inc.
670 Kingston Rd.
Pickering, Ontario
   L1V 1A6
(807) 839-2111

Rawlinson Garden Seed
269 College Rd.
Truro, Nova Scotia
   B2N 2P6
(902) 893-3051

Richters
Goodwood
Ontario L0C 1A0
(416) 640-6677

ENGLAND

David Austin Roses
Bowling Green Le.
Wolverhampton WV7 3HB
Albrighton
(090) 722-3931

Chiltern Seeds
Bortree Stile, Ulverston
Cumbria LA 12 7PB
0229-581137

Roses du Temps Passé
Woodlands House
Stretton, ST19 9LG
(0785) 840217

Tools and Accessories

These companies all have something for the flower arranger, be it a cutting tool or a container.

UNITED STATES

Brookstone Company
5 Vose Farm Rd.
Peterborough, NH 03458
(603) 924-7181

Cherchez
Front St., P.O. Box 550
Millbrook, NY 12545
(914) 677-8271

Clapper's
1125 Washington St.
W. Newton, MA 02165
(617) 244-7909

Country Casual
17317 Germantown Rd.
Germantown, MD 20874
1-800-872-8325

Country House Floral
   Supply
Box 4086
Andover, MA 01810
(508) 475-8463

Dorothy Biddle Flower
   Supply
HC01, Box 900
Greeley, PA 18425
(717) 226-3239

Frank's Nursery & Crafts
6501 E. Nevada
Detroit, MI 48234
(313) 366-8400
(*call for nearest store*)

Gardener's Supply
128 Intervale Rd.
Burlington, VT 05401
(802) 863-1700

Gardener's Eden
P.O. Box 7307
San Francisco, CA 94120
(415) 421-4242

Lagenbach
P.O. Box 453
Blairstown, NJ 07825
(201) 362-5886

Smith and Hawken
25 Corte Madera
Mill Valley, CA 94941
(415) 383-2000

Winterthur Museum &
   Gardens
Winterthur, DE 19735
1-800-767-0500

INDEX

C. P. Maj